Advance I

"Aspen, Colorado, is one of the most celebrated places in the United States, but like any other community it has its preening airheads, community-minded heroes, political bigots and rip-off artists. What most communities don't have, however, is an alert critic who has seen it all and can write it up. Glenn Beaton is to Aspen as Thornton Wilder was to *Our Town*. He lived there for many years, got to know it all, and finally, in disillusion, abandoned it. This book tells you why."

–Peter Wallison, author and White House counsel to President Ronald Reagan

"I, like 327 million of my 328 million fellow Americans, could not care less about Aspen, Colorado, but Glenn K. Beaton did the impossible. His witty and charming history of Aspen magically makes you care. He takes readers from its silver-mining roots to its ski resort days laughing all the way. In between are visits from Johnny Depp, Hunter S. Thompson, and the 10th Mountain Division. I want Glenn to come back in one hundred years and write the sequel in which liberals are driven away by some Pied Piper."

–Don Surber, retired newspaper man and Substack writer

"Glenn Beaton tells the history of Aspen with grace and bite. Although the history is one of dramatic cultural decline, Beaton displays his wicked sense of humor throughout. Reading the book is a pleasure I greatly enjoyed. Beaton both entertains and instructs, for Aspen's story as he tells it illuminates alarming national trends that threaten our survival. Indeed, I am afraid it may give the avant garde thinkers of my hometown ideas that will hasten its further destruction."

–Scott W. Johnson,
Minneapolis attorney and Power
Line co-founder/contributor

HIGH ATTITUDE

HOW WOKE LIBERALS RUINED ASPEN

GLENN K. BEATON

Published by Bombardier Books
An Imprint of Post Hill Press
ISBN: 978-1-63758-949-6
ISBN (eBook): 978-1-63758-950-2

High Attitude:
How Woke Liberals Ruined Aspen

Cover Design by Conroy Accord

Post Hill Press
New York • Nashville
posthillpress.com

Published in the United States of America
1 2 3 4 5 6 7 8 9 10

TABLE OF CONTENTS

PREFACE

THE TROUBLE WITH ASPEN

For seven years, I wrote a conservative column for *The Aspen Times*. I called it The Aspen Beat. It enraged the local liberal establishment. The wacky-wokey mayor told me to leave town. Others threatened to kill me, which always struck me as funny in a place that wanted to ban guns. Would the murder weapon be a sharpened ski pole? Fentanyl dropped into my single malt?

The threats were not so overt that I needed to call the police. They were more like, "You'd better hope I never see you on the street, a-hole," or "Gee, it'd be a shame if something ever happened to you and your house." But I took the latter threat seriously enough that when I bought a new house, I set up a limited liability company to hold the title without my name on it. I never made restaurant reservations in my own name—I did not want them to know who I was until after they had prepared my food and served me. I made a point of using an old, fuzzy photo for my column mugshot. Even so, I became recognized around town. One afternoon, I returned to my car in the parking lot at the downtown grocery store to find my windshield smashed.

The comment section to my column in *The Aspen Times* was routinely filled with so much vulgarity that a decent person dared not click into it. If I pointed this out to the editors, they would usually remove the vulgar comments but not always. When they did, it sometimes took them several days.

The threats and vilification culminated one Christmas Eve when the editor at *The Aspen Times*, without warning or discussion, sent me his own little piece of hate mail. It was an email terminating my column. Safely crouched behind his keyboard three blocks from my house, he chided that "your column no longer represents the values we hold."

Ah, the Left's values—sacred totems they do not just have but bravely "hold." The Left always frames a disagreement with the Right not as a policy issue but as a matter of values. They have them, they hold them, they exhibit them, and they, they imagine, are magnificent—even as they couch them in vulgarities.

I moved to Aspen in 2009 after retiring early from a large international law firm that had a Denver office. Our family had vacationed in Aspen for years and owned a vacation house there. I threw myself into the place. The Sunday cacophony from the church two doors down the street initially annoyed me but later became an important part of reinventing myself. I put some of my lifetime of Colorado climbing experience to work by joining Mountain Rescue Aspen.

And I read the local newspaper. I learned that the reporters, editors, and staff of *The Aspen Times* are uniformly liberal and that both their opinion pages and news pages were slanted that way. But they traditionally had a token conservative columnist. After I had lived there for a few years, I befriended the person writing the conservative column, and she invited me to write a guest column. My piece was more philosophical than political. It was about a recent mass shooting by a deranged teenager and what the incident said about our crumbling culture.

Readers liked it, and I started writing more guest columns. After a half year, a position opened, and the paper invited me to fill the spot.

I was supposed to be a faint and lonely counterpoint to the newspaper's ordinary leftie fare. But my column caught on and grew very popular, or at least very clicked. It often out-clicked front-page news. When it was picked up by national publications like *RealClearPolitics*, it generated far more clicks than the rest of the newspaper combined. For that, the editors never once congratulated me. In fact, it seemed to bug them.

Many of my topics were related to national politics. I applauded the Republican wins in 2016, along with the new administration's approach to the Middle East, energy, and immigration. As a retired lawyer who had argued before the Supreme Court and other federal courts, I especially liked the Republican judicial appointments.

Although my positions were usually at odds with the newspaper's editors and reporters, I was not invariably on the hard right. For example, I wrote that President Trump was unnecessarily polarizing. I also wrote that abortion is a human tragedy to be avoided but that I would not criminalize it prior to fifteen weeks. And unlike most conservatives, I am opposed to the death penalty.

No matter. The Aspen establishment decided that because I was unwilling to toe the leftie line, I was from the wrong tribe. Aspen is not just liberal—and is not liberal at all in the classic sense. It is instead tribal, leftist, incestuous, intolerant, and, importantly, very conscious of image and fashion. It is something like the modern Democratic Party but more so.

The leftie community of Aspen consists of two parts, the rich people and the un-rich people. There is nothing in between. The rich people are disproportionately from Hollywood and the rest of the entertainment industry, along with Wall Street and the rest of the finance industry—including or perhaps especially their divorcées.

Such people are often obsessed with public perception. Aspenites flatter themselves in saying that what attracts people to Aspen is the winter skiing, and what keeps them there are the glorious summers. The summers are indeed glorious, but the winter skiing, while excellent, is not as good as, say, Alta and might not even be the best in Colorado.

What really attracts people to Aspen—at least these particular rich people—is the safe fashion statement, and what keeps them there is the same thing. *Aspen* is right up there with Prada and Givenchy as impractical and overpriced brands but safe ones.

These fashionistas private-jetting to Aspen pack their chicness into their Gucci bags. Indeed, they never leave home without it. When they arrive, they want to display it, along with their jets, their trophy wives or girlfriends, their new skis, their $1,100/day ski lessons, their ability to ski fast on easy slopes, and—of course—their "values."

(But they don't venture near the bumps or the powder. I once rode the lift with a Hollywood actor right after a great snowfall where I was in powder heaven. He was enraged that the snowcats had not groomed all the deep powder into tame corduroy. He fumed, "When I'm payin' $170 a day, I expect the slopes to be properly prepared!")

The political battles in Aspen, as in any liberal battlefield—from the Democratic convention to the streets of San Francisco to the grass of Harvard Yard—are on the left flank. Liberals see the Right and the middle as illegitimate, so the only way to win their approval is to outflank them on the left. Other than a few nutjob exceptions, for example, Democrats never really wanted to abolish the police. They just said so to win their endless I'm-further-left-than-you competition among themselves.

Like lefties everywhere, the lefties of Aspen cling to the belief that their leftist displays are edgy. Leftists in America control academia, Wall Street, most corporate boards, the entertainment industry, philanthropy, the media, most book publishing, almost all social media, and countless Thanksgiving dinner discussions. But they preposterously display their supposed edginess—an edginess that they share with herds of like-minded sheep. They pretend this is still the '60s and that they are rebellious teenagers. If you believe these poseurs, all hundred million were at Woodstock and Selma.

In literature, Aspen leftists love one-time local resident Hunter S. Thompson, a lousy writer who was self-absorbed, self-promoting, self-deceiving, and self-killing. More about him later.

In art, they lavishly funded an art museum that was an abstract laughingstock adorned with an $800,000-a-year director (more than the Guggenheim pays) whose main qualification was that she was someone's daughter (a someone who went to prison for tax fraud). They demanded that *The Aspen Times* apologize for my column critical of her and the museum.

In music, they are destroying the beautiful harmony built by the founders of the Aspen Music Festival over the course of decades by playing race quota games. More on that later too.

In politics, they think a balanced panel discussion is something like two of Joe Biden's alphabet people on the left and former Rep. Paul Ryan on the "right." Their conspicuously, comically far-left politics surely exceed what they really believe and practice at home. As in the rest of fashion, political fashion is based on posturing and flamboyance for public consumption, not opinions and analysis for personal convictions. It is not designed to solve problems but to virtue signal.

As for the people who are un-rich, many moderate ones have self-selected out of paradise proper, including myself. (I now live in the unfashionable purgatory known as "Down Valley.") The leftist, hypocritical, hateful rich drove us out.

The remaining un-rich people are mostly in taxpayer-subsidized housing. They are on the housing dole. To the extent they were not on the left to begin with, life on the dole drove them there. Public welfare has that effect.

The result is a beautiful but dysfunctional town. It is every bit as dysfunctional as Chicago or Seattle. It takes many years to permit and build a house, even though or perhaps because subsidized housing is a sacred goal advocated by the incompetent class warriors on the city council—along with the 45 percent of city residents occupying that housing.

Aspen is even worse than Democratic-controlled big cities in that there is no accountability for the politicians in Aspen. That is because so much tax revenue is generated by soaking the rich that they will never run out of other people's money to toss around. This soaking of the rich is consensual so long as it comes with a spritz of Aspen cachet.

The current mayor of Aspen is a guy with a single legal name—Torre—whose credentials for overseeing the town's quarter-billion-dollar annual budget are that he is a tennis instructor and a staunch advocate of subsidized housing. A city councilman named "Skippy" agitates for the legalization of more drugs. The mayor who told me to leave town is known for crashing private parties, taking swings at eighty-four-year-old men, and cursing women in the park. Of course, he has resided in taxpayer-subsidized housing for decades, which he got for pennies on the dollar.

A series of Pitkin County sheriffs have called for the complete legalization of all drugs. The Drug Enforcement Administration distrusts them to the point they keep impending drug raids secret from them for fear that they will tip off the dealers.

In my newspaper columns, I railed against all this, especially the sacred cow of taxpayer-subsidized housing for "qualified" residents. The program was created decades ago to provide inexpensive housing for service industry workers, such as ski patrolmen and restaurant workers. From those modest and well-intentioned beginnings, the program has ballooned into a never-ending, never-enough multi*billion*-dollar boondoggle.

This gravy train now benefits not so many ordinary workers but privileged insiders. The income cutoff is $300,000 a year. Many of the residents are influencers like *The Aspen Times* editors and reporters. Many others are not even in the workforce because they have been retired for decades.

These upper-middle-class insiders get multimillion-dollar in-town or even slope-side houses and condos for dimes on the dollar. They commonly rent them out in violation of the program rules for tens of thousands of dollars, which is seldom reported on their tax returns.

The program is so metastasized that it includes many of the local poohbahs in addition to *The Aspen Times* editors and reporters. At one point, the mayor and four of the five city council members were on the subsidized housing dole. They tell the rest of us with a straight face that their freebies benefit not them but us because it affords us the privilege of their company.

When I met these types, as I regularly did in this small town, I would do as I was taught when meeting someone. I would tell them my name and offer them a handshake. It was not unusual for them to turn away and refuse the handshake. When I went to sell my last house in Aspen, some realtors advised me to conceal my identity until after closing.

I am glad to say not everyone was so intolerant. Apart from the establishment, many ordinary liberals around town told me that while they usually disagreed with my column, they always wanted to read it because it entertained them and often made them think.

But the mission of *The Aspen Times* and the rest of the Aspen establishment is not to make people think. It is to make people *herd*. They do not want to report the news; they want to cheerlead local leftism. One of the other columnists—which is to say one of the unread and unreadable ones—has declared me "un-Aspen" for refusing to join their squad.

Readers frequently told me they had sent letters to the editor supporting my column or my positions. The paper usually did not publish those letters, but they invariably published the ones that criticized me, even though they typically did so in illiterate and illogical terms.

According to their script, if I dared to express the "wrong" opinions, I was supposed to do so badly and blandly so that nobody would read me except to ridicule me. I was supposed to be the Washington Generals to the liberals' Harlem Globetrotters. I was never, ever supposed to win an argument.

But The Aspen Beat did win. And that is what got it canceled. In short, the newspaper canceled the column not despite its success but because of it.

Many people were reading my column not to attack or mock me but to agree with me, to be persuaded by me, or at least to be entertained by me. Everyone, of course, loved my mockery of Vail, the ski suburbia strung along I-70 on the other side of a mountain range from Aspen. (I wrote that Vail literally gives me hives, and it does.) They liked my admiration for Caitlyn Jenner. They respected my tribute to a fellow volunteer on Mountain Rescue Aspen who died in an avalanche. They even declined to hate my suggestion that men should act like gentlemen.

But from the standpoint of Aspen's hard left, even those columns were problematic. That's because they gave me credibility in enticing readers to read and consider other opinions they normally would not. These included my opinions that perhaps we should not pressure people to vote if they lack the desire or knowledge to do so, that we were asking too much of the Supreme Court and undermining our republic in asking them to formulate policy that is rightly the task of the people's elected representatives, that jazz music might have been less great if Black musicians had been promoted on the basis of their skin color rather than their musical genius, that it is foolish, dangerous, and undemocratic to let your tribe—conservative or liberal—do your thinking for you.

In short, I was not properly playing the token role for which the newspaper had retained me. I was not a laughable object of ridicule. I was a dangerous force of persuasion. For that, the editors, reporters, and staff of *The Aspen Times*—Democrats, Marxists, or Stalinists to a person—had to cancel me. They had to shut down my forum as an opinionist when I successfully advanced the wrong opinions.

They deny this, naturally. In that same termination email, the editor assured me, "We will continue to have a conservative voice in our paper, but we want one that better represents the local base and does not go off on name-calling, wild assumptions and are [sic] based off a false premise."

The token "conservative" they engaged to replace me got off on the wrong foot by announcing at the outset that she was not one. Of course not. Having learned from their experience with me, the newspaper would not have taken her on if she were. But tokens are not supposed to reveal that they are tokens.

In the eyes of Aspen lefties, she partially redeemed herself in her first column by proclaiming that what Aspen really needs is... more taxpayer-subsidized housing.

As for my alleged "name-calling," "wild assumptions," and "false premises," the editor chose not to elucidate. Not then, nor during the previous seven years when *The Aspen Times* had published nearly two hundred of my columns without objection by this editor or his predecessor.

He concluded his email not with thanks for my seven years of free writing (I had always declined their stipend) but with a gracious, "you are welcome to take your column elsewhere."

That permission was not only unneeded but insincere. The other Aspen newspaper is part of the same hard-left Aspen crowd, as are newspapers throughout the Roaring Fork Valley. And *The Aspen Times* was owned at the time by a chain of twenty-seven newspapers located in small mountain towns of Colorado and the West, so they, too, were out. I had effectively been canceled from at least thirty newspapers.

I thought about shutting down my laptop. But in my previous life—my real life as a lawyer—it was writing that I enjoyed most, followed, in roughly this order, by court appearances, dealing with clients, timekeeping, and mandatory continuing legal education, where I was forcibly injected with the American Bar Association's latest political pablum while they pretended to teach me updates on the Federal Rules of Civil Procedure.

I'm also a political junkie. Plus, I think I'm funny.

I decided to continue my column as a blog. It is not hard to do. You can rent space at WordPress, Substack, or elsewhere for practically nothing. Then all you need are readers and something for them to read. I had both.

I gave my blog the same name as the byline I had chosen at *The Aspen Times*. It is called "The Aspen Beat." You can still subscribe at theAspenbeat.com or at Substack, and, as of this writing, it is still free.

My readership from *The Aspen Times* quickly migrated to The Aspen Beat. I also increased the frequency of my column to about ten a month. Liberated from the cloister and Kool-Aid of *The Aspen Times*, my writing became unleashed, unreined, unfettered, undiluted, unshaven, unkempt, unplugged, and unapologetic.

The blog took off and now dwarfs the little newspaper that fired me. My first piece described my Christmas Eve massacre. It was picked up by six or seven national outlets and generated tens of thousands of clicks. In comparison, the entire circulation and click count for *The Aspen Times* was a fraction of that on a good day, and my column had been responsible for many of those.

Meanwhile, karma came calling. *The Aspen Times* publishes an annual "Best Of" competition each autumn where its readers vote on such matters as "Best Bartender," "Best Restaurant," "Best Realtor," and so on. One of the categories is "Best Columnist." The marquee category is "Mr. Aspen."

The 2020 competition came around nine months after I had been fired on Christmas Eve in 2019. The readers of *The Aspen Times* voted me "Best Columnist," even though—or perhaps because—*The Aspen Times* had fired me the year before. When the competition rolled around again in 2021, they voted me "Mr. Aspen." That was gratifying, to be sure, and I thank my readers for that.

But I tell my story and the story of Aspen for a broader lesson. Bias and corruption are not just the product of out-of-touch newspapers whose trust ratings are near zero. It is not just by uneducated leftists living in taxpayer-subsidized slope-side digs who demand free stuff while lacking any math skills beyond the concept of "more." It goes deeper.

Democrats outnumber Republicans at least three to one in Aspen. Absent accountability to opposing viewpoints, the hard-left media, the limousine liberals, and the local leeches are intertwined in a soiled, stinky, incestuous bed.

This is not unique to Aspen. Small, rich, and beautiful towns—towns that were a paradise in the past and could be again—have been radicalized into something resembling Venezuela or Cuba, except with more money to push people around. Something similar has also happened to America's big cities. Why is that?

In short, Aspen's ills are bigger than Aspen itself. Aspen is a canary in the coal mine of western civilization, a leading indicator of where the rest of us may soon be headed.

As Barack Obama liked to say when he was about to scold someone, this is an opportunity for a "teaching moment." I will try to teach in what follows, but—trigger warning!—there will also be some scolding.

CHAPTER ONE

SILVER BOOM, SILVER BUST: ASPEN IN THE EARLY DAYS

Explorer, surveyor, and army Colonel Ferdinand Hayden conducted several surveys of the Rocky Mountains, including in 1872, the first government survey of the area that became Yellowstone Park. The next year, his team explored to the south in the Colorado Territory.

Leadville, at the headwaters of the Arkansas River in central Colorado, was already booming with gold mining. What lay to the west over difficult, fourteen-thousand-foot mountains and twelve-thousand-foot passes of the Continental Divide and down into the valley of the Roaring Fork River was mostly unknown except to fur traders and nomadic Ute Indians.

Hayden went there. In a journal entry that changed Colorado's history, he noted that the terrain, rocks, and perhaps the geology looked like that of Leadville. Hayden's 1873 survey planted the seeds of Aspen, though his journal was not published until five years later.

Hayden also noted and photographed a high peak with a horizontal ledge bisected by a central couloir. They were snow-filled and formed a cross shape. He dubbed the peak "Mount of the Holy Cross," and the 14,011-foot peak is still named that. The local electric company in the Roaring Fork Valley is "Holy Cross Energy," a name that rankles some people as inappropriate for a public utility company.

For all of Hayden's naming of the features of the western landscape, not much was named for Hayden in return. One thing that does bear his name is 13,561-foot Hayden Peak near today's Aspen, so named by Hayden's men.

Early ski pioneers two generations later seriously considered building their new ski facilities on Hayden Peak rather than on Aspen Mountain. The result would have been a much different Aspen. The ski runs of Aspen Mountain terminate practically in downtown Aspen, while Hayden Peak is half a dozen miles up Castle Creek outside of town.

If Hayden's men had been prescient enough to foresee the ensuing mining, skiing, and frolicking in store for Aspen, they might have assigned his name to what is now Aspen Mountain. If they had, he would be famous today.

But perhaps not in a way he would have liked. For all his accomplishments as a surgeon in the Civil War, a tough and intrepid explorer in midlife, an officer in the army, and then a geology professor afterward who helped establish Yellowstone as the nation's first national park, he was a modest and scholarly man. Not much honors him apart from lesser mountains and the town of Hayden, Colorado, which has a population of 2,452. Native Americans have called for Hayden Valley in Yellowstone to be renamed on the grounds that Hayden "advocated for the extermination of tribal people who refused to comply with federal dictates." Little in the historical record supports this allegation, but do not be surprised if geographers soon cave to the mob's demand that Colonel Hayden be canceled.

Western commercial interests and politicians put Hayden's exploration to practical use. They had learned something in the California gold rush of 1849 and then again in the Colorado gold rush of 1859, which centered on Leadville and other mountainous areas east of the Continental Divide. They learned that mining booms are good for business. In the 1870s, they engineered another.

Silver dollars had long been coined in the United States. United States mints were required to coin silver brought to them by private parties, a practice that was called "free silver." People who wanted a looser money supply liked the free silver policy because the amount of money in circulation was continually increased simply by the act of mining silver. People literally minted money for themselves by bringing their mined silver to the mint to be coined. It was the nineteenth-century equivalent of the modern Federal Reserve's quantitative easing. From a private perspective, it was even slicker than that because, apart from the mechanical operation of the mint, it could be accomplished outside the government. And it was perhaps more economically sound than quantitative easing because, unlike the Federal Reserve's supply of paper money, the only limit to which is the speed of their printing presses, the supply of silver ore is finite.

But in 1834, Congress messed with the money supply. They effectively devalued the new silver currency by increasing the amount of silver required to produce a given denomination of the coin. It suddenly took more than a dollar's worth of silver to make a silver dollar. Unsurprisingly, silver bullion owners largely stopped making their silver into dollars.

In 1873, Congress demonetized silver to officially end the coinage of silver as US currency. Gold coinage was in circulation all this time, and the Treasury held substantial gold reserves. The Treasury strove to increase those gold reserves to shore up the paper dollar during and after the Civil War. The net result of all this was plummeting world silver prices.

Various interests campaigned for a return to free silver policies, including farmers—and there were a lot of farmers in those days—seeking an expanded money supply in the economy to buy their crops and a few western senators who held stakes in silver mines. They pushed legislation through Congress in 1878 requiring the Department of Treasury to purchase large quantities of silver to make coinage to use in combination with the long-standing gold coinage. Leadville's silver deposits became more profitable, and Leadville boomed for the second time.

In that same year of 1878, probably not coincidentally, Hayden's 1873 survey of western Colorado was finally published, describing the geology over the high peaks west of Leadville and down into the Roaring Fork Valley. Hayden's descriptions enticed miners over the Continental Divide in epic three-week treks on foot, horseback, and wagons to assay the ore on the other side.

Today's geologists are not surprised that these intrepid miners discovered huge silver deposits in the geologically complex Roaring Fork Valley. Numerous mining towns popped up, such as Independence at about 11,400 feet with 1,500 residents at its height, Ashcroft, Ruby, and one called Ute City. All that remains of these towns are a few rotten timbers, except Ute City. That one was renamed a year later "Aspen."

Aspen, too, nearly went bust. It was so remote that it was difficult economically to bring in supplies and to bring out silver ore. The construction of a rail line in the late 1880s saved the town. An old railbed is now a paved bicycle path extending all the way to Glenwood Springs, forty miles down the valley at the junction of the Roaring Fork and Colorado Rivers.

Blessed with some of the biggest silver deposits on earth and equipped with a rail line to ship it out, Aspen thrived. In its heyday, it supplied one-sixth of the country's silver and one-sixteenth of the world's. The Smuggler Mine unearthed the world's largest silver nugget, a one-ton behemoth the size of a modern shopping cart.

Hydroelectric power was generated for the mines, electric street lights were installed, a water system was constructed, and a trolley line was built down Main Street. A tramway was constructed partway up Aspen Mountain to the mines near the path of the present gondola. The town had six newspapers, and they did not all have the same conventional and correct political viewpoints.

The population topped twelve thousand, compared with today's seven thousand. It would have been higher if 1,500 Ute Indians had not been relocated to Utah.

Some of Aspen's early success was due to good fortune, some of it was due to bad acts, and some of it was just ugly. The presence of silver in and around Aspen was, of course, pure luck. The demand for silver, engineered by Congress's mandating silver purchases and coinage by the Department of Treasury, was bad crony capitalism. The deportation of the Utes was ugly. But the rest of Aspen's early success was the product of raw, unbridled, risk-taking entrepreneurialism.

Aspen was not planned. It started as a high-altitude and high-attitude tent town of miners, who undertook outrageously difficult and hazardous jobs underground on the dim chance that they might strike it rich but usually did not, and their suppliers, who usually did become prosperous but also not rich.

None of them thought the world owed them a living. They had little patience for claim jumpers, outlaws, drunks, or whores. Wyatt Earp and Doc Holliday were acquainted with the place—Earp arrested a murderer in Aspen, and Holliday died of tuberculosis down valley in Glenwood Springs, where he is buried in an unmarked grave in an obscure hillside cemetery—but Aspen was never a shoot-'em-up town until Spider Sabich and Claudine Longet arrived a century later.

There were no taxpayer-subsidized houses, no class struggles, no chicks with dicks, no Hollywood types, no Black Ski Week, no billionaires, no Gay Ski Week, no global warming fretting, no global celebrity feting, no private jets, no equity, no virtue-signaling lawn signs, no Music Festival, no Ideas Festival, no Food and Wine Festival, no Jazz Festival, no Beer Festival, and no Arts Festival.

No, these early Aspenites had little time for the festivities of festivals. They worked for a living. Thomas Hobbes might have been describing an Aspen silver miner whose life was indeed "solitary, poor, nasty, brutish, and short." And he lived that life mainly in the dark amid poisonous fumes.

A notable exception was Jerome Wheeler, a wealthy eastern businessman who was president of Macy's. In a transplantation typical in the history of Colorado, Wheeler visited the state, fell in love with it, and moved there. He went to Aspen early in the silver boom and invested in the mines. It was a good investment for a while. He built the Wheeler Opera House, still standing, and the Hotel Jerome, which is still among Aspen's finest after half a dozen remodels. He liked to name things after himself.

Congress's tinkering in the monetary system was just getting started. In 1890, they passed the Sherman Silver Purchase Act, expanding the government's purchase of silver for coinage by another 50 percent. But the result was a decline in the Treasury's gold reserves, which sparked a financial panic. Congress swiftly repealed the act in 1893.

The repealing legislation came at the worst possible time for the silver market because the artificial demand produced by the legislation had generated a western mining boom from Colorado to California. They were mining far more silver than the industry could absorb without the prop of Treasury Department purchases.

The price of silver crashed by one-third in what came to be called the "Panic of 1893" (though it was called "the Great Depression" until the 1930s). Mines in Aspen, Leadville, and throughout the West closed. Over half the employable men in most mining towns were abruptly out of a job.

It was government interference with markets—specifically the government propping up the silver market—that birthed Aspen. Perhaps fittingly, it was additional government interference—the government's untimely undoing of its propping up of the silver market—that nearly killed it.

To ordinary miners, all this commodity market manipulation by an arrogant, corrupt, and stupid government two thousand miles away was no more understandable than it was to the local deer or to the Ute Indians who had been carted off to Utah. All they knew was that it became a lot harder to scratch out a living.

Jerome Wheeler declared bankruptcy. He did not get a bail-out. For the second time, Aspen nearly became a ghost town, and by the early part of the twentieth century, the population was down to five hundred.

CHAPTER TWO

COWS, POTATOES, AND GHOSTS: THE QUIET YEARS

After the silver bust, there was practically nothing. A couple of the mines near Aspen reopened briefly but even those closed in the '20s. The biggest thing to hit Aspen at that time was an influenza epidemic. It was called something politically incorrect under current standards: the Spanish Flu. We now know that name was probably epidemiologically and geographically incorrect as well—it likely originated in Kansas.

This "Kanish" Flu killed fifty to one hundred million people in a world with less than one-third of today's population. It was as if COVID-19 were to kill a couple hundred million people rather than its actual toll of about seven million. Most died in a four-month period in late 1918. In cities, corpses were stacked in the streets like cordwood.

Of those fifty to one hundred million deaths, some were among the remaining residents of Aspen. Lockdowns did not happen in those days, though in the case of that particular flu, they might have done some good. Unlike COVID-19, the flu hit young and healthy people as hard as the weak and elderly.

The prized trolley line on Main Street was torn out in this sleepy period, but several agricultural irrigation ditches were dug in the nearby hills. The fleeing population abandoned houses in town. Remodeled gems selling for $15 million in today's swanky West End could be had then for practically nothing.

Aspen, during those years, became less urban and more agricultural. The main cash crop in the thin mountain soil was potatoes. Cattle ranches were also scattered here and there. Farming and ranching were not particularly profitable, though. Aspen sits at nearly eight thousand feet in elevation. Winters are long, cold, and snowy, and the growing season is short. The limited rail service made crop and livestock delivery outside the immediate valley impractical. Aspen was an isolated, barely alive outpost in the high Colorado Rockies. You'd have been foolish to bet on Aspen in those days.

Farmers, ranchers, and poor people are not and were never known as a cool, freaky, or fashionable crowd. Like the miners before them, they did not have time for festivals—except for an occasional rodeo. The farmers' market back then did not sell bad artwork or cheap souvenirs or arugula or free gawking at the best MILFs on the planet, as they do now. They sold—hold onto your hat!—potatoes.

There were no celebrities or billionaires or even millionaires. There is no record of any gays or transsexuals within one hundred miles. It is likely that many people were born, lived, and died without seeing a skier or a Black person, much less a Black skier who is encouraged to break the rules.

That does not mean Aspenites were simple-minded or bigoted. In contrast to modern Colorado cities like über-woke Boulder, there is no record in Aspen of the Ku Klux Klan, for example. Missing was the racial, ethnic, and religious strife that plagued much of the country in the Jim Crow days. St. Mary's Catholic Church in downtown Aspen is surely more a target of the "tolerant" today than it was of the intolerant in the early twentieth century.

The absence of racial and ethnic conflict in Aspen was undoubtedly due, in part, to the forced relocation of the few remaining Utes two generations earlier. That relocation was probably inevitable. Like most indigenous people of the time, the Utes were a violent and warring society. Interaction between Ute and non-Ute tribes, and even between competing Ute tribes, often took the form of raids to enslave children, rape women, collect warrior scalps, and steal guns and horses—the Utes were masterful horsemen. Sometimes they raided to prove their manhood, sometimes for revenge against a tribe that had raided them, and sometimes just for fun. The word "Comanche" is Ute for "enemy."

These characteristics do not mean the Utes were "bad." It means they were typical nomads of the nineteenth century.

Today's local lefties in Aspen feel very badly that the Utes were carted off to Utah to be confined to reservations where raiding was rare and scalps were scarce. Part of that guilt is rooted in a Pollyannish belief that the Utes had been living in harmony with nature, whatever that means, until aggressive, racist, capitalistic whites invaded their traditional lands.

But these local lefties are not suggesting that the Utes' land be given back to them. That land is now worth trillions. Giving the land back to them would be too expensive.

So, the Aspen lefties instead do what lefties always do in such circumstances. They salve their guilt about things that people with white skin did hundreds of years ago to the ancestors of today's Utes, not by helping today's Utes but by ostentatiously feeling sorry for them. Feeling pity makes rich liberals feel noble, and it is very inexpensive. If only the stores on the Ute reservations over in Utah would take Aspenite pity in payment.

Back to 1918. Jerome Wheeler had declared bankruptcy decades earlier, and his finances never recovered. That year, he died at the height of the epidemic, and his Wheeler Opera House was seized by the city for $18,000 in unpaid taxes.

The city still owns and operates the Wheeler as a theater. Like most government operations, it operates at a loss. Aspen subsidizes it with a 0.5 percent real estate transfer tax, which amounts to a lot at Aspen real estate prices. The city makes a show of throwing money at the theater—they are very good at throwing money—but even they are unable to spend the money as fast as it rolls in. The fund now has over $40 million in reserve.

They do not have opera at the Wheeler Opera House anymore, and the theater tends to be politically correct Kabuki. You will not find Dave Chappelle performing there. But it is still a grand place to see a movie so long as you're not in the mood for something deemed deplorable and semi-fascist like J. R. R. Tolkien.

In fact, it may soon be the only place in town to see a movie. The city's ongoing and extravagant subsidizing of the Wheeler nearly drove the town's only private theater out of business in the early 2000s. Unable to compete effectively, they sold off a good portion of their building and halved their seating.

Jerome Wheeler's passing marked the loss of the biggest, baddest, best, and last business mogul of the early days. The other kind of mogul—the ski kind—had not yet appeared. But to a keen observer, there were signs.

CHAPTER THREE

SNOW IS THE NEW SILVER: THE BUSINESS OF SKIING IN ASPEN

To understand Aspen, you must first understand a little about skiing. I have been skiing since the days the boots were leather, the bindings were cables, the pants were jeans, the jackets were army surplus, the lifts were slow, and the ticket was seven dollars. Skiing and I grew up together.

Skiing per se is not a big business. The annual revenue of Aspen Skiing Company (called "SkiCo" by locals) is only around $100 million, and the total employment is only around one thousand. At least in the West, ski companies seldom own their slopes but rather lease them from the Forest Service. What they own are just lifts, buildings, and a name.

The mountain operations pay poorly. Seasonal patrollers, lift operators ("lifties"), snowcat operators, and on-hill restaurant workers get lousy pay and lousy benefits. If you think it is glamorous, try standing in the snow at a lift for six hours, helping a giggling gaggle of beginners on skis place themselves on a wooden bench that is traveling toward them at what they perceive to be about eighty miles per hour.

There is more money and fun in teaching the sport. Ski instructors can do OK if they establish a well-heeled clientele that tips them generously. But even the well-heeled clients often are not in the mood to give a big tip to the instructor after paying his employer $1,100 for the day's lesson of six hours minus lunch. Some instructors are not expert skiers, though they may be good instructors. In either event, they and their client get to cut the lift line, which saves time and feels grand. For years, the SkiCo instructor uniform resembled a marching band outfit, but they recently upgraded them.

While ski resort companies are not large by Wall Street standards, neither are the resorts where they operate. The one thousand employees of Aspen Skiing Company make it far and away the largest employer in Pitkin County, where the population is less than twenty thousand. It is the dominant force in the local economy. SkiCo has clout in the Valley.

Where a ski company can make real money is in ancillary businesses, especially real estate. Industry behemoth Vail Resorts brings in about $2 billion a year in revenue, but a good part of that is through its synergistic real estate development business.

Vail and Aspen are different in that way, as in so many other ways. Vail was created out of thin air in the early '60s. The founders leased the ski mountain from the Forest Service and bought the ranchland at the base on the cheap. Since then, a huge part of their business has been real estate development. Depending on how you do the accounting, Vail probably just breaks even on mountain ski operations. The business model is something like a golf course development. The golf course is a loss leader for the lucrative housing development.

SkiCo has never had the real estate business of Vail. Like Vail, they inexpensively lease the mountain, but the land at the base of Aspen's ski mountain was already taken. It was a town at the time skiing took hold. But you cannot argue with SkiCo's success. It has gotten richer from snow, image, and its limited real estate business than Aspen miners ever did from silver.

SkiCo's riches are more a product of being in the right place at the right time rather than being hardworking or clever. In a macro sense—a geographic sense—this right place lies just west of the Continental Divide. Storms moving west to east, as they typically do, drop their snow as they rise over the Divide. That snow amounts to a few hundred inches a year. The elevation of the ski slopes ranges from eight thousand to twelve thousand feet. The cold, dry air produces light, fluffy snow, which is much easier and more fun to ski on than the dense snow of New England or Europe.

The snow is easy, but the terrain is not. Aspen Mountain has zero beginner slopes. The intermediate and expert slopes are steepish and often treed. Numerous accidents happen on Aspen Mountain, including deaths. I was once run into by a skier at high speed, which is more common than it should be. There is easier terrain at nearby Snowmass or Highlands, both also owned by SkiCo (though those mountains also have some terrain that is harder than anything on Aspen Mountain). But it is Aspen Mountain that visitors who ski about eight days a year want badly to ski and want to ski badly. "Skiing Aspen Mountain" is what impresses the guys back in the office. The result is a lot of intermediate skiers barreling down the deceptively steep slopes of Aspen Mountain at a velocity much higher than safety permits. Aspen ski patrollers usually look the other way.

In the fashion sense that is crucial to today's Aspen, this right place for skiing is the one that captured the attention of the glitterati, partly by design and partly by happenstance. Atlantic City and Galveston three generations ago were not exactly hotbeds in a changing culture focusing more on outdoor recreation. Somewhere had to become the playground of the new outdoorsy celebrities, but it could have been many different places. To some extent, Aspen just got lucky. And with it, so did SkiCo.

Once the Aspen brand became a prestigious one, it did what prestigious brands naturally do: it became even more prestigious through little effort by the brand owner. Brands take on a life of their own. They become famous for being famous. In the business of vacation resorts, the brand "Aspen" is now one of the strongest in the world.

"Brand" is used here in the casual sense, not the legal trademark sense. Neither SkiCo nor anyone else owns "Aspen" as a trademark. It's a geographical place that goes back 150 years. This can be contrasted with "Vail," which was a coined name by the founders of the Vail resort in the early '60s and was owned by them as a registered trademark until their rights were finally invalidated in a lawsuit in the early 2000s—a lawsuit that I personally lost in representing Vail. Imagine if "Aspen" were a legal trademark that could be licensed for royalties.

Skiing caught on in America in the '60s and '70s, and Aspen rode the wave. In view of the natural advantages of Aspen for skiing, the branding of Aspen that occurred in the early refounding in the '50s and '60s, the vision of the founders, and limitless luck, it was impossible for SkiCo not to succeed.

Once they did, their business success begat more business success, just as their brand success begat more brand success. In the business world, they hit the big time in 1978 when they were bought by 20th Century Fox. This undoubtedly contributed to the reputation of the place as a celebrity hangout.

Then, in 1981, flamboyant billionaire Marvin Davis bought 20th Century Fox in a buying spree where he also scooped up the Beverly Hills Hotel and Pebble Beach Resort. Being owned by Marvin Davis and having sister brands like Beverly Hills and Pebble Beach did not hurt the Aspen brand.

SkiCo was then bought by the Crown family in the mid-'80s. The Crowns are the descendants of Henry Crown, who began with a sand and gravel company. His descendants built it into a conglomerate that acquired General Dynamics, which the family still largely owns. The extended family is now worth perhaps $10 billion, with other interests in companies like Continental Illinois Bank, Maytag, Hilton Hotels, and the Chicago Bulls.

Politically, the Crown family is diverse. The patriarch, Lester Crown, formally endorsed Barack Obama. But his daughter Susan Crown and her husband have been known to host Karl Rove and other conservative figures for gatherings at their Aspen home.

So that is the natural, business, sports, and cultural setting of Aspen. It is the milieu into which an improbable group of World War II veterans and a Chicago industrialist pitched their idea for refounding Aspen after World War II.

CHAPTER FOUR

SOLDIERS OF FORTUNE AND THE REPUBLICAN BOX KING

Wooden skis invented in Eastern Europe in prehistoric times found use in Aspen from the outset. In the winter of 1899, it snowed every day. Modern skiers would celebrate a winter where every day was a powder day, but the few remaining miners in 1899 were probably less giddy. Skis were the only way of getting around town.

The turn of the century saw downhill skis come into use. Skiing became not just a way to get through the snow but a way to have fun. Even before World War II, people for amusement were hiking uphill for the sole purpose of sliding back down on slippery boards. By the 1930s, downhill skiing was a sport in Aspen.

But it required a lot of effort, as anyone knows who has tried to hike or ski up a snowy hill. Even modern uphill skiing on alpine touring or "AT" skis, with snow-grabbing adhesive skins on the bottom, involves exhausting exercise while gasping for breath at high altitudes with sweat dripping off your nose—all while your toes freeze. Skiers had to "earn their turns," as AT aficionados say. This limited skiing then and still limits uphill skiing now.

Skiing in Aspen changed forever in 1937 with the construction of the town's first "boat tow," a looped cable running partway up Aspen Mountain, around a wheeled bulwark, and back down. It was powered by a reclaimed Ford Model A engine and could pull an eight-person boat-shaped sled up the mountain one sled at a time. Skiing was suddenly not just for athletes. Some athletes still stubbornly ski uphill even today, and you can run into them on the slopes—hopefully not literally, but that does happen. But for the genteel, skiing has been downhill ever since.

One of the pioneers behind Aspen's early ski industry was Billy Fiske, an Olympic bobsledder from a Chicago banking family. Fiske wanted to build a ski resort in the Rockies after seeing the Swiss resorts where he competed in the Olympics. He saw the skiing potential of Aspen after being presented with photographs by a miner seeking investors. Fiske turned down the offer to invest in the mines but bought some property for nearly nothing to build a ski lodge.

Fiske staffed his new venture with Andre Roch, a rugged Swiss skiing and mountaineering expert. Roch was later part of the 1952 Mount Everest expedition that came within one thousand feet of being the first to summit. His daughter died in a climbing fall that would have taken Roch as well if the rope between them had not snapped. Roch was an avalanche expert, but he and a son were once swept away by one. Roch saved the son with forty-five minutes of furious digging, which prompted his most memorable quote: "The avalanche doesn't know you're an expert."

Roch's expertise and Fiske's money produced a racing slope on Ajax called Roch Run. It was considered one of the premier racing slopes in the world. The Roch Cup was later won by such notables as Billy Kidd and Franz Klammer.

World War II both paused and altered the course of skiing in Aspen. The Tenth Mountain Division, a light infantry unit of outdoorsmen recruited and trained in part by the National Ski Patrol, was stationed nearby in the ghost town of Ashcroft for a time before moving closer to Denver. Soldiers saw the boat tow on Aspen Mountain and saw the snow conditions and terrain in the vicinity. They remembered it all, and, like Fiske, they saw potential.

The enemy dubbed the soldiers of the Tenth in their white winter combat camouflage "White Death." The Tenth certainly dealt more death than they suffered, but still, nearly a thousand were killed in combat, and another three thousand were injured. One casualty gravely wounded in battle was not a mountain man but a Kansan named Bob Dole, who went on to become a Republican senator and presidential candidate. He said the skis and skiers of the Tenth saved his life.

After the war, some veterans of the Tenth came back to Colorado with big ideas. One who did not return was Billy Fiske, who died from injuries suffered in the Battle of Britain. He flew as a Canadian because the United States was not yet formally in the war.

Those who did return included Friedl Pfeifer, an Austrian skier who had emigrated in 1938 to escape the Nazi occupation. In his desire to become an American citizen, Pfeifer joined the army, and they naturally assigned him to the Tenth, where he first saw Aspen. He lost part of a lung in combat in Italy but finally made his way back to Aspen after the war in 1945.

Another was Pete Seibert. A New England prep school graduate, Seibert joined the army, was assigned to the Tenth, and was badly injured by a mortar shell in Italy. Like the other Tenth soldiers, he saw Aspen and its potential and returned after the war to become a ski patrolman. Seibert founded Vail in the '50s and spent the rest of his life just one mountain range away from Aspen.

Percy Rideout was a Dartmouth graduate who learned the degree did not guarantee much of a living. He wound up on a trail crew in Sun Valley, where he met Pfeifer. He was drafted in 1942 and assigned to the Tenth. In Italy, he was shot through the cheek leading an assault on Riva Ridge. He was awarded the Bronze Star, the Silver Star, and the Purple Heart.

Although both were in the Tenth, Rideout and Pfeifer lost touch during the war. They met up again in Colorado Springs after the war while awaiting discharge.

Johnny Litchfield was another Dartmouth grad and a world-class skier in downhill, Nordic, and especially ski jumping. He was the other notable ski pioneer from the Tenth. Pfeifer recruited him, along with Rideout, to run the ski school immediately after the war.

As famous as he was for skiing, Litchfield became just as famous for founding Aspen's most notorious restaurant, the Red Onion, which continues serving hearty fare to this day under different ownership.

Unlike Litchfield and most other Aspen skiing pioneers, Rideout did not stay long in Aspen. Feeling the financial pressure of a wife and new child in 1947, he left Aspen and the obscurity of skiing for his wife's home in Nebraska, then took a job in California with an agriculture company. Rideout never shared in the riches from the creation of "Aspen" out of Aspen.

The final piece of the puzzle came in the person of Walter Paepcke, the Chicago industrialist who put up money for the venture. Paepcke's German immigrant father had founded a lumber mill and related companies. His son, Walter, was bright, ambitious, and not humble. He noted in his prep school yearbook that only one college would be graced by his attendance. He chose Yale.

Either because he was indeed an exceptional student or because they were tired of his conceit, or both, Yale permitted him to graduate early. He later inherited his father's businesses and business acumen and built Container Corporation of America, a very successful box and packaging company often abbreviated CCA.

At the outset of Paepcke's career in the '20s, goods were still being shipped to retailers in wooden crates and on pallets. The retailer would empty the crates and unload the pallets, shelve the loose goods, and sell individual units off the shelf. Somewhat counterintuitively, Paepcke thought goods could be made more attractive to customers by enclosing them in packages. He once observed that "almost every product has by its very nature either form, shape, color, design, composition, printing, or something which can generally be grouped as a subdivision of art." He conceived of the idea of packaging goods individually with eye-catching graphics. He was decades ahead of his time in anticipating the thrill felt by today's customers in opening the box.

Paepcke was naturally attracted to graphic arts. He liked the New Bauhaus movement brought to Chicago by German immigrants with whom Paepcke shared a cultural heritage. The spare simplicity of Bauhaus appealed to his sense of a package's form merged with its function. He supported and was influenced by Bauhaus designers for the rest of his life.

Paepcke's vision in graphic arts, together with his shrewd management, carried the company through the Great Depression, and he emerged after the war stronger than ever. By the '50s, his company had today's equivalent of about $2 billion in annual sales.

Paepcke was a Republican who viewed the New Deal as unjust and unconstructive government interference in the market. His companies and plants were sometimes the targets of government labor-enforcement actions. Frustrated with what he viewed as heavy-handed government meddling, he moved many plants and operations offshore to Latin America and elsewhere.

For at least his American workers, however, Paepcke was an enlightened boss. His company buildings were festooned with artwork. He offered stock options and a company-wide pension plan. Much of his company was unionized. He favored liberal arts graduates because he believed that a broad education in the humanities—back when that was what a liberal arts major got—was a good foundation for what he would later teach them about the packaging business.

His interest in packaging, as loosely defined, extended to his way of presenting his company to the public—his public relations "package." He revolutionized communications with shareholders through readable and graphic-laden reports. He once commissioned a study to understand the demographics of his shareholders in the hope of attracting more.

He recognized that his influence on the public's perception of his company was limited because his customers were not the public who bought the goods in the boxes he sold. His customers were instead the manufacturers who bought his boxes to package those goods. Boxes are not exactly a glamorous consumer product. To the degree he made them so, it was to enhance the public's perception of the goods inside. Most people had never heard of Container Corporation of America and did not care to.

Paepcke was nonetheless concerned about the public's perception of CCA. It is not known whether that was due, in part, to his and his wife's German heritage at a time when Germans were unpopular or even hated. In any event, in deference to the nature of his business in selling to companies rather than to consumers and the pedestrian nature of his product—packages—his public engagement strategy was subtle.

He created an advertising series called "The Great Ideas of Western Man." Once a month, the series ran print advertisements interpreting "Syntopicon," which was an index to Encyclopedia Britannica's collection "Great Books of the Western World" that had been written by his friend Mortimer Adler. The only mention of Paepcke's company in these advertisements was an inconspicuous logo.

Syntopicon never became as popular as Adler had hoped. But Paepcke's use of it was widely acclaimed—not so much by consumers of the goods he packaged but by his real customers, the sophisticates in corporate boardrooms and marketing departments deciding what the packages containing their goods for sale should look like and who should manufacture those packages.

Paepcke, and by extension Aspen, owed much to Paepcke's wife, Elizabeth. The daughter of a romantic languages professor, she was a finishing school graduate who later studied drawing and painting at the Art Institute of Chicago. She worked as an opera costume and set designer and for an architectural firm. Through her father, she was friends with Mortimer Adler, and it was she who introduced Paepcke to him. She was instrumental in arranging an Art Institute of Chicago exhibit of advertising art prominently featuring CCA called "Modern Art in Advertising."

Elizabeth started vacationing in Aspen in the 1930s. An athletic person, she rode a wagon partway up Aspen Mountain and skied down. She was smitten.

She talked Walter into a Memorial Day visit to Aspen in 1945, just as the war in Europe was ending. The town was empty, as it often still is on Memorial Day, or "mud season," as the locals call it. They reported that on one walk, they saw only three people. All three were drunk.

But Walter was as taken as Elizabeth by the beautiful terrain and the potential for a resort. He bought as much property as he could, typically just by payment of its back taxes. And he met with Pfeifer, Litchfield, and Rideout. Paepcke and Pfeifer created Aspen Skiing Company and hired Litchfield and Rideout as their first ski instructors.

SkiCo was thus created by three war heroes—two of whom had been badly injured in combat—and a Republican business tycoon who was the son of a German immigrant. They weren't woke; they were dreamers. And they had the appetite for risk and hard work that makes dreams come true.

CHAPTER FIVE

THE GERMAN CULTURAL INVASION: HOW THE PAEPCKES REINVENTED ASPEN

Aspen's first chair lift, as distinguished from the bumpy little boat tow, opened in 1947 as one of the longest in the world. For Europeans, at least, who were accustomed to great skiing in Switzerland and Austria, suddenly Aspen was on the map as a premier, if distant, ski destination.

In America, skiing was an obscure sport. The powder skiing of Utah was far in the future, ski equipment and clothing were primitive and challenging, and skiing was too expensive to attract a middle-class consumer in those days of limited airplane travel. But Aspen was very well positioned for the later ski boom and was already prospering compared to the quiet and boarded-up years it endured before the war.

For Walter and Elizabeth Paepcke, the skiing was mostly bait for bigger fish. From the outset, they envisaged Aspen as a cultural stage more than a ski town. Neither was an artist, but both were patrons of the arts. They liked art, architecture, music, and literature, and they liked artists, architects, musicians, and writers. And they liked people to know they did.

Aspen, at the time, was a remote, dilapidated outpost of dirt streets, boarded-up houses, and a few poorly stocked stores. The Paepckes' plan to make it a Chautauqua-in-the-Rockies for art, ideas, and intellectualism was either brilliant or risky—they were either genius or lucky—or both. Whatever it was, they were proven correct.

Elizabeth, the daughter of the romance languages professor who had spent her life in and around literature and art, was more artistically educated than Walter, the son of a businessman who had spent his life building that business into one of America's great corporate conglomerates. But he, too, became sophisticated in the arts with the help of his money, his brains, his unconfined interests, his wide circle of intellectual and artistic friends, and Elizabeth's contacts and tutelage.

They brought to Aspen another Chicago acquaintance, Austrian-born Bauhaus designer Herbert Bayer. Bayer went on to live in Aspen and influence design there and everywhere for decades. He was responsible for the Bauhaus design of the Aspen Institute's campus at Aspen Meadows.

They also brought their two daughters to Aspen on the old tortuous and serpentine gravel road over Independence Pass, which tops out at an elevation of 12,400 feet. The story is told that on his descent from the top of the pass toward Aspen, Walter stopped at 11,000 feet at the ghost town of Independence, nearly at the elevation of timberline. He exited the car and announced to the daughters amid the rotting log ruins that they had arrived in Aspen. The daughters cried until dad told them he was just kidding. Perhaps Paepcke was not just being humorous but also managing expectations. After seeing the high ghost town of Independence, the girls probably thought Aspen looked pretty good.

While Pfeifer ran the emerging ski operation, the Paepckes turned their attention to matters of taste. One fell right into their laps.

A group of intellectuals, including Paepcke's friends at the University of Chicago, had an idea to honor Johann Wolfgang von Goethe on the two-hundredth anniversary of his birth in 1749. They thought the German romantic was a good topic for their intellectualizing because they were somewhat romantic themselves, and the world's postwar view of German culture could use a little romance.

They found sympathetic ears in the Paepckes, both of whom were of German heritage, had spoken German in their homes as children, often spoke German between themselves even then, and were romantics at heart even if they did not know it. The pair were enthusiastic about a Goethe celebration from the outset. Never mind that one of the Chicago intellectuals promoting the idea was a fervent advocate of one world government just a few years after another German had started a world war to achieve exactly that.

These Germans from the City of Broad Shoulders hatched a three-week event in the summer of 1949 called "The Goethe Bicentennial Convocation and Music Festival." It attracted two thousand guests to Aspen. To run the event, Paepcke created a nonprofit he named the Aspen Institute for Humanistic Studies, later shortened to the Aspen Institute.

Albert Schweitzer was one of the speakers the Paepckes and their German friends in Chicago persuaded to come. It was three years before the great Franco-German theologian, organist, humanitarian, and philosopher was awarded the Nobel Peace Prize. Although it was his first and only visit to America, he was already well-known worldwide. His presence drew *Time* magazine and *Life* magazine to cover the event.

The Paepckes lodged Schweitzer in their own home. They puckishly reported to friends that he was a difficult guest who played the piano at all hours—aware, of course, that there are worse things than being kept up at night by Albert Schweitzer's piano playing.

For the musical concerts, the Paepckes rented a big-top tent with enough capacity for two thousand people and set it up in a meadow that had been a horse track. They purchased the meadow by paying back taxes, as they purchased much of their Aspen real estate holdings. About a mile from downtown, it was only a twenty-minute walk for downtown guests through the picturesque though still somewhat rundown West End. The music was mostly German fare. Schweitzer gave a talk in German and another in French.

The event lost about $30,000, which was no small amount at the time, but the publicity was priceless. The Paepckes and their collaborators talked about next year even before the festival ended. In preparation, Paepcke bought the rented tent.

The next year's festival honored two more Germans, composer Richard Wagner and Johann Sebastian Bach, on the two-hundredth anniversary of the latter's death. The Paepckes turned to their friend Mortimer Adler to outline a series of talks and roundtables. The opening seminar focused on Adler's favorite philosopher, Aristotle.

Adler later spent most summers in Aspen. He wrote that Aspen is proof that "in the scale of values, the Platonic Triad of the true, the good, and the beautiful takes precedence over the Machiavellian triad of money, fame, and power." At the time, he was right.

The musicians at the first festival were enthralled with summertime Aspen. The following year, about three dozen accomplished music students and their teachers came. The year after that, the music part was formalized with the creation of the Aspen Music Festival and School.

The Festival and School ultimately attracted world-class musicians from around the globe. Aaron Copland was a composer-in-residence in 1975. Duke Ellington performed in 1975, and John Denver performed accompanied by classical musicians in 1980. Cellist Yo-Yo Ma performed in 2013.

The summertime weather of Aspen is perfect, especially for someone coming from the South, East, or Midwest. The high temperature is usually in the upper seventies, and a sweater is necessary for evening alfresco dining. The occasional afternoon rain shower passes before you can get your slicker on. Today's summer sidewalks still feature impromptu street music—mostly classical but with some jazz—by world-class musicians playing for tips.

Ellington and Ma notwithstanding, it was noticed a few years ago, after decades of stunning success in attracting and helping train terrific talent from around the world, that the great majority of classical musicians and composers at this classical music school—as in all other classical music schools—were classically white. You can guess what happened then. More about that in a later chapter.

Walter Paepcke died in 1960, but his extraordinary wife Elizabeth lived until 1994, dying at age ninety-one. In her house in the West End, next door to Jack Nicholson, she became the grand dame of Aspen. After a visit, Andy Warhol wrote in his diary, "I met this beautiful lady in her 80s who looked like Katharine Hepburn."

She was not only beautiful but also loved to play, drink, and tell a bawdy joke. She warned, however, that leisure "should concern itself with those things we do to replenish the spirit, such as listening to music, watching good films or theater, taking part in discussions of politics and ideas. It is the opposite of killing time." According to historian James Sloan Allen, she and Walter believed in moral discipline, social responsibility, hard work, and restraint.

Walter died while the dying was good, but Elizabeth lived long enough to see Aspen start down a sordidly different path in the '60s. Goethe, Bach, Bauhaus, Schweitzer, and Aristotle gave way to moral relevance, promiscuity, drugs, conspicuous consumption, class-based strife, and materialism at both ends of the class spectrum.

It all peed on the blossoms of intellectual humanism that Elizabeth and Walter had planted and nurtured. Elizabeth told a reporter in the '80s that the town had "become a town of glitz and glamour...a nut without a kernel. My heart is broken."

The emerging glitz and glamour were bad enough, but the anti-glitz and anti-glamour were worse. Walter had often told

Elizabeth and his colleagues that he wanted "no riffraff" in Aspen. In 1960, the year Walter died, Hunter Thompson came to town, in his words, "drunk as a loon."

CHAPTER SIX

FEAR AND LOATHING: THE SIXTIES COME TO ASPEN

Aspen and the rest of America changed in the '60s, in some ways for the better but mostly for the worse. America recovered, but Aspen never did.

The change in Aspen was marked by the arrival of a rich, tawdry celebrity culture. Nouveaux riche financiers and Hollywood types replaced intellectuals and artists. They brought with them a different morality. The place became infested with New Age crap whose adherents denied the relationship between causes and effects. This mysticism later deteriorated into wokeness, where feelings substitute for logic.

Hunter S. Thompson was symptomatic of this decline. Thompson was a part-time sportswriter for a small-time newspaper in Florida and a member of the air force. They tossed him out in 1960 (honorably, it should be noted) after his superiors complained that he had an independent streak that seemed to rub off on other airmen. He was a troublemaker. And he was broke.

His 1960 Aspen trip was simply to ferry some stuff for a friend in exchange for a few dollars. He returned in 1963 for a short time with a pregnant wife but then quickly left for California.

Thompson's life changed with the publication of his 1967 book *Hell's Angels*. To gather material for the book, he lived with the Angels for a year. Given their propensity for display—exhibitionism is not too strong a term—it is probably no surprise the Angels were happy to pose for him. He probably learned a thing or two about self-promotion.

The Angels eventually figured out that Thompson was using them for book material, and they demanded a share of the profits from the book. That led to the type of incident the Angels were known for—they beat him nearly to death. That's when he decided he had enough material. He stopped participating in the group and started writing about them.

His book still sells today. It is not deep, but it is entertaining in the same way its author was. His readers were, and are, mostly young men who enjoy stories of motorcycles, machismo, fighting, drinking, drugs, adolescent male bonding, and dare-devilry. And abusing women. Thompson's casual treatment of gang rapes by the Angels remains controversial, at best.

In 1967, after the publication of the book, Thompson came back to Aspen for good—and bad. He rented a house in Woody Creek, an old ranching outpost eight miles from town that later became something like an Aspen suburb. Woody Creek and other real estate down the Roaring Fork River from Aspen is referenced by Aspenites a bit snidely as "Down Valley." By Aspen standards, Down Valley is inexpensive and, therefore, inferior, or maybe even tacky, but by the standards of the real world, it is none of those things.

Woody Creek is still known to outsiders for the presence of Thompson's favorite watering hole, the Woody Creek Tavern, a place that, these days, caters more to boomers on electric bikes than to ranchers on horses while still striving, maybe a little too hard, for its lost authenticity.

From his Woody Creek house and probably the tavern, Thompson continued writing. He felt he had been compensated poorly for *Hell's Angels*, apparently because the publisher merely paid him what their contract called for, but he ultimately made real money in 1971 with *Fear and Loathing in Las Vegas* and other "gonzo" books.

His books might today be characterized as participatory or reality journalism. Tom Wolfe later described Thompson's style as "part journalism and part personal memoir admixed with powers of wild invention and wilder rhetoric." In truth, his books are often enjoyable reads but are not journalism at all. They are exaggerated, melodramatic, staged portrayals in which the writer is one of the characters orchestrating events with an eye toward the storyline. The books sometimes contain a nugget of truth and sometimes do not. Truth by the nugget or otherwise was never Thompson's objective.

Thompson liked a line attributed to William Faulkner—with whom Thompson had practically nothing in common—and paraphrased years later without attribution by an unapologetic Dan Rather after being caught fabricating stories about George W. Bush's military record: "The best fiction is far more true than any journalism."

Maybe, but not when the fiction is presented as fact. That is not journalism; that's fabrication. It is unethical, and when it's about a person, it's libelous. Thompson's stuff would not have been liked by Faulkner or any other real writer. Thompson's approach can be summed up with, "Lies are OK if they serve the cause." The cause was to sell books.

Thompson was indeed good at selling books. He knew how to draw attention to himself and his writing. He especially understood the power of image and branding. He was not the first to use the term "gonzo" to describe his style of participatory journalism, but he knew a good trademark when he saw it.

His play with guns was real enough. He kept a huge cache of them. He referred to his one hundred acres in Woody Creek as his "fortified compound." He liked to play there with not just guns but also dynamite. He admired Karl Marx. A poster of Che Guevara hung in his kitchen.

He theorized, unburdened by any facts, that the 9/11 attacks were conducted by the US government but that proof was "difficult" to obtain. Why it would be difficult to prove something that hundreds or perhaps thousands of people would have been in on is one of those questions that conspiracy theorists never have an answer to.

One episode of the elaborate reality shows that Thompson orchestrated for his life, or maybe just for book material, was a run for sheriff of Pitkin County in 1970 after he had lived in the county for all of three years. He ran under the "Freak Power" ticket.

His platform included a lot of musings about drugs, a subject with which he had considerable familiarity. He once said, "I hate to advocate drugs, alcohol, violence, or insanity to anyone, but they've always worked for me."

In point of fact, he didn't hate to advocate those things at all. He loved to and was doing so in that very statement. He loved the attention it brought him—at the expense of foolish people who took his clowning seriously.

In his campaign for sheriff, his drug policy was nuanced, to put it generously. He proposed to decriminalize drug use but not trafficking. It is unclear how users were supposed to obtain their newly decriminalized drugs if not from traffickers. And he proposed putting criminal traffickers of drugs not in prison but in public stockades, but only if their drugs were of poor quality. The common thread of these policies was that they were attention-getting.

Less nuanced but also attention-getting, he proposed banning any building that blocked mountain views. Or perhaps that proposal was just BS since it would be a land-use move that is not within the power of the Pitkin County Sheriff's Department. Law was not the forte of this candidate for sheriff; publicity and selling books were.

Not all his proposals were off the wall. He suggested banning cars from Aspen, for example. Aspen, even today, has only about three blocks of pedestrian malls—far less than Vail, the place over the mountain range that Aspenites like to deride as tacky, and nothing like European resort towns such as Zermatt, where cars are completely banned within thirty miles of town.

It has always been the locals in Aspen who object to car bans, even as they rail against the evils of cars. Most visitors are fine with a car ban because they routinely stay in the middle of town within walking distance of everything, including the ski gondola, and they would prefer not to be run over in ski boots on slippery streets with their own skis and kids' skis in hand. But, no worries, the local greens, who won't give up their cars, still show their colors by making a show of fining customers who use plastic bags at the grocery store.

Just before the election, Thompson showed up at the office of *Rolling Stone* with a six-pack of beer as a prop, declaring that he was about to be elected "Sheriff of Aspen." There is no such thing, but the "Sheriff of Pitkin County" probably didn't have the right ring. He wrote a piece for *Rolling Stone*, which it published under the title "The Battle of Aspen" under the byline "Dr. Hunter S. Thompson."

Thompson had purchased his "doctorate" for twenty-five dollars from a mail-order church. He never received a legitimate doctorate, master's, undergraduate, or even high school degree. In fact, he was kicked out of high school after being sentenced to sixty days in jail for robbery. That was after he had been kicked out of the high school literary club for previous "criminal activity." Perhaps he—and *Rolling Stone*—intended his byline as a spoof on doctors or writers or magazines, but of course, Google-less readers of the day had no way of knowing that.

Thompson later said that the *Rolling Stone* piece energized his opponents more than his supporters. It is not clear whether he thought that was good or bad or that he even cared. What mattered was that people read it.

Thompson won the vote in Aspen but lost the county-wide vote by a few hundred votes.

One thing about his reality show journalism was true. He did not take care of his mind or body, and it showed. Drugs, alcohol, violence, and insanity didn't work so well for him, after all. His career peaked shortly after *Fear and Loathing*, back in the mid-'70s, and it fell apart over the next thirty years.

His excuse was that he could no longer do the writing he once did because he was too well-recognized to embed himself anonymously into a setting. This complaint was odd coming from someone who had always gone to lengths to draw attention and be recognized by his appearance, actions, and writing.

In 2005, at age sixty-seven, with his health fading and his career all but over, he telephoned his wife from his "fortified compound." While on the phone, he blew his brains out as his son and daughter-in-law chatted in the next room. They did not come to his body immediately because they mistook the gunshot for a bottle falling on the floor, something that apparently happened with some frequency.

Thompson thus joined the many suicide perpetrators/victims of Aspen, a place where the rate is about double the national average.

Thompson left a suicide note of sorts. It reads:

> "No More Games. No More Bombs. No More Walking. No More Fun. No More Swimming. 67. That is 17 years past 50. 17 more than I needed or wanted. Boring. I am always bitchy. No Fun — for anybody. 67. You are getting Greedy. Act your age. Relax — This won't hurt."

Thompson was probably right that his end did not hurt—not him anyway. The hurt to him was in everything prior to that. History has not recorded whether Thompson ever met Elizabeth Paepcke or Mortimer Adler. If so, the meeting was probably short.

One person he did meet was Johnny Depp, who lived in Thompson's basement for a while to gain insights for his role as Thompson in an upcoming 1998 film adaptation of *Fear and Loathing in Las Vegas*. Depp arranged the funeral at Thompson's place in Woody Creek.

Given the Aspen setting, it could have been called the "Thompson Funeral Festival." Thompson had carefully planned and scripted the whole show in advance—except, predictably, how to pay for it, which he left to Depp. The highlight was when his ashes were shot into the air by a cannon perched on a 153-foot tower, as Thompson instructed.

Depp still idolizes Thompson, even after paying for the funeral show and paying the estate a million dollars for hundreds of boxes of probably worthless paraphernalia and unpublished writings—some as pedestrian as notes, recipes, and shopping lists. While Thompson cultivated a devil-may-care image, he imagined that such things were worth hanging on to.

To justify to himself his expenditures on Thompson's funeral and junk, and maybe to hype the value of the junk, Depp gushed on a YouTube video that "he's as original as Kerouac, or Ginsberg or Walt Whitman or Bob Dylan."

Depp's comparison is telling. Whitman, Kerouac, Ginsberg, and Dylan are known for carefully cultivating their public image of originality. A cultivated image of originality is not exactly an oxymoron, but it is in the neighborhood. Depp is right that Thompson did that, too, but the difference is that Whitman, Kerouac, Ginsberg, and Dylan were also immensely talented writers.

When President Richard Nixon died, Thompson said something that is not on a poetic par with Whitman, Kerouac, Ginsberg, or Dylan:

> "If the right people had been in charge of Nixon's funeral, his casket would have been launched into one of those open-sewage canals that empty into the ocean just south of Los Angeles. He was a swine of a man and a jabbering dupe of a president. Nixon was so crooked that he needed servants to help him screw his pants on every morning."

Narcissism is too generous a term for Thompson. Narcissism is a blameless psychiatric condition that cries out for treatment. Thompson was just an uneducated, mediocre writer who discovered he could sell books and be famous by becoming part of a wild and semi-factual story. His glamorization of his behavior probably messed up the lives of some of his naive readers who were unaware that much of it was an act. He himself said he was never sure whether he should adopt the persona of one of his book characters in public, as people anticipated, or his real persona.

I never met Thompson, but I suspect that his real persona of a troubled, self-made, attention-seeker with a knack for telling a semi-factual story was probably less entertaining but more interesting than the fictional book persona of wild, vulgar, and druggy. Thompson was not fearful or fearsome. He was loathing and loathsome.

It is fitting that his final attention-grabbing story was the Thompson Funeral Festival that he put Depp up to. The predictable and intended result was undoubtedly that he sold a few thousand more books.

Apart from the additional book royalties, he would have been pleased to see that the audience to that show included 280 notables, such as John Kerry, George McGovern, Ed Bradley, Charlie Rose, Jack Nicholson, John Cusack, Bill Murray, Sean Penn, Lyle Lovett, and John Oates.

People instinctively like a rebel. Maybe that's because they go through life subordinate to The Man. And so, they identify with someone who prides himself on giving the finger to The Man. In the '60s and '70s, that instinct was a dominant feature of American culture.

The best I can say for Thompson is that he gave the finger to The Man—or at least pretended to. For the rebel wannabes of Aspen, that was enough to win him a majority of the votes for Pitkin County Sheriff and to mythologize him in a way that has survived his self-inflicted death.

But he was not a real rebel. Real rebels have a cause. Nathan Hale lamented that he had but one life to give for his country, while Thompson gloated that he had one life to give for his personal self-promotion.

This phony was the model for the subsequent fake edginess of Aspen and its elites. Predictably, safely, and in unison, they imagine that, at great personal risk, they are creatively and independently giving the finger to The Man.

But in the year 2023, in Aspen, they themselves are The Man. The Man they make a show of giving the finger to is The Man of the 1950s, long extinct. And many of them give the finger to him only *after* becoming rich.

At Thompson's funeral festival, one of the attendees was a nobody named Bob Braudis, a charismatic, hulking, gap-toothed transplant from Boston who grew up dreaming of becoming a western sheriff—and became one.

Braudis came to Aspen to be a ski instructor after working at Dun & Bradstreet and arrived in time for Thompson's campaign for sheriff. He volunteered to help, and the two became buddies. When Aspen had a dry ski year in the mid-1970s, and his marriage broke up, Braudis joined the sheriff's department as a deputy to support himself and two daughters.

Braudis's upbringing was as conventional as his early stint at Dun & Bradstreet. He was not from the school of hard knocks. He was upper middle class and educated. He stood out for his physical appearance and size but mostly did not court controversy. He generally got along with people. He was popular around town and hard not to like personally.

Braudis adored Thompson, perhaps because Thompson exhibited a wildness and grittiness—even if manufactured—that Braudis himself had not known. In interviews, Braudis played down his ordinary family background and conventional Wall Street career and played up his counterculture cred:

> "I was part of the movement of my generation, which was anti-war, pro-civil rights, pro-women's rights—whatever any social justice in the '60s was. I was straining to get out of the corporate rut and into that. So what did I do? I bailed

> out and moved to Aspen and got stoned. And it was all good."

Ah, another self-proclaimed rebel. There is no more evidence for Braudis's boast that he was a '60s rebel than there is for Joe Biden's boast that he was a leader in the civil rights movement. Braudis was not a hippie in Berkeley or anywhere else. And the only street life he knew was as a dweeb at Dun & Bradstreet.

Braudis said about Thompson's books, "The message was that as a civilized society we had peaked and we were on the back nine of that golf course. Things weren't going to get any better."

But from the time Braudis was referring to—the '70s and '80s—until now, things did get better in the world. Pollution is way down, the population bomb has been defused, wealth is up in all parts of the world and across all income groups, starvation is nearly eradicated, most disease is being conquered, racial strife has lessened, women's opportunities have increased, and technological breakthroughs are astounding.

Count on progressives always to be blind to progress—it does not fit their doomsday narrative, their satisfying self-aggrandizement, or their search for a low-risk, low-effort cause (global warming, anyone?) on which to rest their manufactured rebellion. But life is not golf, humanity is not on the back nine, and after what they've put us through, the Left doesn't deserve a mulligan.

The conventional sheriff who defeated Thompson in 1970 was replaced by a less conventional one who, in turn, handpicked Braudis to replace him in 1986. Braudis won the next election and brought even less conventionality to the office, perhaps inspired by his ongoing friendship with and adulation of the faux-edgy Thompson.

Pitkin County Sheriff's office personnel report that they never saw Braudis use drugs, and Braudis himself said he and Thompson had an arrangement such that Braudis was never "compromised."

Maybe so, but it is documented that Braudis disappeared for a time in 2006 and turned up at a rehab clinic. Moreover, he certainly tolerated drug use by others, including his good buddy Thompson.

Braudis's public position on drugs was one of tolerance and looking the other way. He viewed drug abuse of all kinds, including fentanyl and heroin, as a medical issue, not a legal one.

It was not always that way in Aspen. The Aspen Police Department ran an undercover drug operation for a few years in the early '70s. They hired an undercover agent to infiltrate the loose drug culture in town, which wasn't difficult. Then he busted his druggie friends. He later joined the Aspen Police Department as a beat cop but was ultimately driven out of town. Like drug users everywhere, the ones in Aspen do not like snitches.

In contrast to Braudis's view that his job was something grander than enforcing the drug laws, the United States Drug Enforcement Agency was specifically tasked with enforcing those laws. They believed Braudis's office was not trustworthy and expressed that distrust in a concrete way. When it came to Pitkin County, they discontinued their standard policy of giving local law enforcement courtesy alerts about impending drug raids for fear that the target of the raid would be tipped off. This amounted to an implied accusation that the Pitkin County Sheriff's Office employed one or more drug felons and accessories, though the accusation was never formally made.

Braudis was sheriff for twenty-four years, until 2006. He died of natural causes in 2021 at age seventy-seven.

Braudis's approach to drug abuse was defensible, but the defense is ultimately not a good one. It is based on a philosophy quite contrary to the overall leftism that drug users typically embrace. It is based on libertarianism—the notion that people are entitled to make their own decisions about such things as drugs (but not politics or religion) because, after all, they're grown-ups.

Except that some are not. Braudis was casual about enforcing drug laws, not just around town, where he dealt with people who were grown up, more or less, but also in a place where they weren't—the schools. There are good reasons not to allow children to drive, drink, smoke, abuse drugs, or elect genital mutilation surgery.

Braudis's libertarian approach to individual drug use also failed to consider the societal effects. Aspen, unfortunately, became a case study illustrating those effects.

Not only did drug use in Aspen explode, but so too did some of the users. In 1984, a federal raid on the house of alleged drug kingpin Steven Grabow found drugs and $1.4 million in cash. The Aspen police chief said he was not told of the raid until the day it happened. The soft-on-drugs sheriff guy—who later hired Bob Braudis—maintained that he was not told about it at all. Somebody was apparently told, however, because it was reported that the perps were tipped off.

Grabow was indicted by a Denver grand jury the next year, and a trial was set on charges that he was dealing $35 million annually in Aspen. A month before the trial was to begin, he finished a tennis game in Aspen, returned to his car, turned on the ignition, and a bomb blew up under his seat. The murder case was never solved.

Others took Grabow's place. In the mid-'90s, a DEA informant reported that cocaine was frequently and openly dealt at a particular apartment complex, with as many as eighteen transactions a day being conducted. The informant wore a wire, and many deals were recorded.

A subsequent raid by forty federal, state, and local agents confiscated a meager amount of drugs—about forty-four grams of cocaine and a bit of crack. They also seized what looked like a plastic bag of heroin that would have had significant street value, but analysis showed it to be flour.

The dealers may have been tipped off about this raid, too, by one or more of those forty agents. They may have secreted their cash and drugs elsewhere, then filled the bag with flour to taunt the cops. Some twenty-four people were arrested, but only four served time.

By the early 2000s, cocaine was openly dealt in Aspen. Two restaurants were notorious drug-dealing havens, Cooper Street Pier and the venerable Little Annie's Eating House. The Aspen Police Department led a raid on the two restaurants.

The assistant chief, who headed the raid, told reporters that asking where cocaine could be bought in Aspen was considered a stupid question. Everyone knew where. He told the newspapers that there were numerous reports of drugs being openly dealt at Cooper Street Pier especially. The reports came from school children, from persons arrested who were found to have cocaine in their pockets, and from concerned citizens.

Several dozen agents and officers descended on the two restaurants simultaneously, some with guns drawn. This time, the DEA and the Aspen Police Department apparently left the sheriff's office out of the loop, and the outcome was more successful. Ten drug arrests were made, plus another eleven immigration arrests. These days the immigrants would be honored, not arrested, and it is doubtful the drug dealers would serve time.

The occasional successful drug bust has not lessened the availability of drugs in Aspen but is simply evidence of it. The drug culture of Aspen—the casual acceptance of drugs not just by habitual users but by most residents and especially by the community leaders—has won.

As the Pitkin County sheriff for twenty-four years, Braudis officially advocated legalizing all drugs, including meth, fentanyl, and cocaine. Braudis got partway there when all of Colorado passed a referendum legalizing pot in 2012. Pitkin County voters favored that referendum by a 75 to 25 percent margin, and the Aspen margin was even, well, higher.

In odd juxtaposition to $20 million penthouses, downtown Aspen is now festooned with pot shops selling marijuana ten times as potent as the old dorm room stuff. Marijuana use is even tolerated on the ski slopes, though SkiCo prefers that you drink since they have a license to sell alcohol but not pot.

Even before the legalization, "Mick" Ireland, while mayor, is said to have implied to visiting school children that pot smoking was OK by telling them they should be careful not to set the forest on fire when they smoke pot in the woods.

As for the not-yet-legalized drugs, Aspenites followed the example of the sheriff. In 2018, a man brazenly went to the police station to claim his lost wallet, which had been turned in there. The police told him they wanted to talk to him about that wallet. According to the police report, he replied, "I bet I know what you want to talk to me about."

The officer said, "What?"

The man replied, "The drugs in my wallet." The man apparently thought recovering his wallet from the police station was worth whatever inconvenience he might incur by admitting that the four grams of coke in it were his.

In 2010, a rash of date-rape drugging incidents occurred. Women were passing out and waking up miles away after being drugged at parties or bars. Some had been raped. Like a scolding schoolmarm, the successor sheriff to Braudis announced that these assaults and rapes were "not acceptable."

Perhaps not acceptable, but also not chargeable. No one was ever arrested.

In 2017, the DEA conducted a raid that netted ten arrests and several pounds of cocaine from perps who dealt in Aspen over a fifteen-year period. The DEA opted to keep both the sheriff's department and the Aspen Police Department out of the loop because, according to the DEA agent, the sheriff had "some kind of relationship" with some of the arrestees. The sheriff initially disputed that but later admitted, "I know three people on that list, and I would not call it a close personal relationship with any of these people."

A few parents and teachers stood against the drug and alcohol culture. The newspapers reported on a woman named Jackie

Long, who started a program seeking to treat teenage addiction after losing her own daughter. She told the city council, "I don't want to say I am proud of this wonderful cocaine resort we have. I want to say I'm proud of a city that has a wrap-around opportunity to help youth and I just don't see it."

A local teacher criticized Aspen's lax enforcement of the drug laws: "The sheriff and police department [just] give lip services to the problem."

Much of the Aspen establishment does not even do that. A city councilman named Skippy wants Aspen to decriminalize "psychedelic drugs," such as ecstasy and psilocybin. His rationale is that these drugs are said to be useful in treating depression and other emotional and mental illnesses.

Other council members seem opposed, but it is striking that Skippy would advocate more drugs in a town already suffering both an image as a drug den and the sad consequences of being one.

When it comes to drugs, people should not always get what they want. Norms, rules, and guardrails are established not by the people at large but by a civilized—some would say privileged—subset of them who get elected for their brains and judgment. Braudis gave in to mob rule, perhaps because he imagined himself a fashionable iconoclast like his buddy Hunter Thompson rather than an enforcer of laws established by wise people over a millennium.

Thompson and Braudis gave Aspenites what they wanted. Thompson's self-centered sociopathy pointed the way to hell, and Braudis's good intentions, along with his misplaced worship of Thompson, paved it. May they suffer the punishment they deserve.

CHAPTER SEVEN

THE WILDING OF ASPEN: HOW THE SIXTIES SPAWNED A SYBARITIC VIRTUE-SIGNALING DYSTOPIA

Aspenites like to believe that their town was a hotbed of anti-war and civil rights activism over the years because they consider that hip. *The Aspen Times* once tried to establish that Aspen was always in the vanguard of progressive activism, but their evidence for the claim was pretty thin.

Their first piece of evidence was a bathtub entered as a float in the 1954 Fourth of July parade by a local gadfly. He was opposed to water in the Roaring Fork River being diverted away from making artificial snow for him on Aspen's ski slopes and through tunnels to Denver for drinking and irrigation. His statement was not exactly inspiring or noble.

The next example was an Aspen protest in 1965 against Humble Oil. But there is a lot less here than meets the eye. The protest was not over pollution, global warming, oil spills, or the habitats of otters. It was over the oil company's desire to build a gas station in the West End. It was a strictly small-time, local NIMBY issue.

It was not until 1967 that any real protest emerged. That year, a few people gathered around a vacation house that then–Secretary of Defense Robert McNamara had rented. Refreshments were handed out. It was not exactly Kent State.

Two years later, a few Aspenites protested an underground nuclear detonation in Western Colorado designed to free natural gas. *The Aspen Times* reported that their protest failed but did generate some great "protest art." How daring. No doubt this art has found its way into the uber-woke Aspen Art Museum.

Other protests were similarly paltry. There was the 1975 protest against the pricing of ski lift tickets after SkiCo excluded Aspen Mountain from the three-mountain season pass package that the locals used and doubled the price in an attempt to chase away the ill-mannered locals who were driving off the well-heeled tourists.

And there was a series of late-century protests against fur coats, which succeeded in enacting a meaningless ban on the sale of fur within city limits. And then there was the horn-honking protest against metered parking.

The Vietnam War and its subsequent parade of progressive causes du jour did not fundamentally change Aspen in the '60s and '70s. For all their talk of social consciousness, it was mostly just talk. The everyday citizens of Aspen have always been unengaged with real social problems. They are more concerned about personal issues like image, property values, skiing, free housing, and outdoor recreation.

Also, indoor recreation—including sex, alcohol, drugs, and their attendant criminality. It was not the progressivism of the '60s but the general American decadence spawned by social and political upheavals that ultimately changed Aspen for the worse.

Start with sex. The sexual revolution is the result of a pharmaceutical one, though it pains today's leftist Luddites to admit it. It is the product of oral contraceptives. Invented in the early '50s, they became commercially available in America in 1960. In 1965, the Supreme Court ruled that states could not ban them, and by the late 1960s, they were very common, as was the rising incidence of promiscuity, infidelity, and divorce. Sex follows contraception like babies follow the absence of it.

Once the possibility of pregnancy was reduced to near zero, the only reason not to engage in sex was that one's elders frowned on it. But any parent knows that disapproving facial expressions only serve to encourage the behavior the parent disapproves of. A good part of the sexual revolution was just old-fashioned teenage rebellion, which the pill neatly decoupled from its natural consequences.

Another but lesser cause of the sexual revolution was feminism. Feminist dogma still sometimes teaches that sexual promiscuity is liberating. And it is—for the man. It is no wonder many men see no reason to get married anymore. Feminism's accidental bias toward men did not become apparent until decades later.

The new culture of promiscuity found a target-rich environment in Aspen. The people attracted to Aspen in the '60s were not staid. Some were intellectuals like the Chicago crowd, some were celebrities and celebrity wannabes, some were artists and musicians, some were ski bums in a day when lift tickets were still only a few dollars, some were service workers looking for a good time, and some were impressionable nouveaux riches seeking to burnish their coolness credentials. None of those are known for their prudishness. Aspen became a place to hook up and, later, to snort up. It became a sexual playground for men—and a sex trap for women.

Most of the resulting hookups are undocumented, as hookups are supposed to be. But a few during and after the '60s have been written up or passed along by word of mouth. To the extent they are known at all, it is often because they occurred in conjunction with illegal drugs or violence. It takes a lot to get arrested for drug use in Aspen. Usually, you have to hit, stab, or shoot someone.

Consider the 2009 Christmas Day assault by Charlie Sheen on his then-wife Brooke Mueller. Mueller called 911 and reported that a high and/or intoxicated Sheen was threatening her with a switchblade and that she "feared for her life." Her story was credible enough that Sheen was arrested and charged.

Sheen pleaded the case down to a misdemeanor, and the judge gave him all of thirty days, minus the time he had already spent in rehab—plus thirty-six hours of anger management therapy, which I'm guessing just pissed him off.

Mueller herself was no stranger to drugs. The authorities often said she had to go to rehab, but she mostly said "no-no-no." When she did go, including once at a Mexican "extreme rehab" facility, it didn't take. Two years after the Christmas attack by Sheen, she was arrested at an Aspen nightclub for possession of cocaine with intent to distribute. The woman is a handful. She has been thrown off airplanes for belligerence, was photographed with a crack pipe, and has been seen pawning her jewelry, presumably for drug money.

In 2019, a man named Joe Lipsey, involved in the trucking and firearms wholesale businesses, was arrested along with his wife for providing cocaine and alcohol to underage minors in their home. Seems the Lipseys hosted rave parties for their son and his friends. Some of the distribution and inhalation were caught on video, but…hmm…the cocaine charges were dismissed for lack of evidence.

Parents throwing drug or drinking parties for their underage children and their friends is a tradition in Aspen. At least two prominent realtors have been so charged, with little effect on their lucrative careers.

Then there is World Cup ski racer Spider Sabich. He lived in Aspen in the mid-'70s with his girlfriend, the French actress Claudine Longet. One Sunday afternoon, Sabich was shot in their bathroom. He bled to death in an ambulance on the way to the hospital. Longet told police that the gun had accidentally discharged while Sabich was showing her how to use it.

In the bathroom.

Longet was charged with murder. Her ex-husband, singer Andy Williams, paid for her defense.

The Pitkin County Sheriff's Office made several procedural errors in investigating the case. Without a warrant, they seized Longet's diary, which suggested that her relationship with Sabich had soured. That was contrary to what she told the police. Also without a warrant, they drew a blood sample from her. The sample showed cocaine. Finally, they mishandled the gun. The gun evidence showed that when Sabich was shot, he was at least six feet away, bent over and facing away from Longet, a position and distance seemingly inconsistent with the act of showing a person how to use a gun. All that evidence was excluded from the trial due to the investigators' errors.

The jury convicted Longet of negligent homicide, and the judge sentenced her to a mere thirty days. She was allowed to choose the days, and she chose mostly weekends. She was also reportedly allowed to paint her drab jail cell in brighter colors. Enduring thirty days of weekends in drab colors as punishment for fatally shooting her lover in the back while he was bent over in the bathroom would have constituted cruel and unusual punishment.

After she finished her "sentence," she vacationed with her married defense attorney. The attorney later divorced his wife and married Longet. The two still live in Aspen but, understandably, in a low-profile way.

In the sex but not drugs department (insofar as we know) is an amusing story about Donald Trump, his former wife Ivana, and his tabloid-friendly girlfriend, Marla Maples. In 1990, Trump and Ivana were vacationing in Aspen. By some combination of design, coincidence, or nefariousness, Marla was also in town. The three crossed paths at one of the on-slope restaurants.

Ivana knew there was another woman and publicly referred to her as "Moola." It was not a term of endearment. When she saw Maples in the restaurant with another woman friend, she asked the woman to tell Maples to leave. Maples overheard the conversation and confronted Ivana, reportedly declaring, "I love your husband. Do you?"

Ivana did not at that particular moment love her husband. She and Trump got into a big argument, which continued and escalated as they left the restaurant. Trump tried to ski away, but Ivana, a much better skier, skied backward in front of him, scolding and wagging her finger. Maples ultimately won Trump, and Trump won the presidency, but Ivana was the best backward skier. Far better than the unfortunate Michael Kennedy.

The sixth of Bobby Kennedy's twelve children, Michael Kennedy, died on the slopes of Aspen in 1998. Skiing very fast and without a helmet, he turned around and skied backward to catch a football thrown by a family friend in one of the reckless games the Kennedys indulged in. He went back-first into a tree and was probably dead before he hit the ground. This happened a year after being accused of having a three-year affair with the family babysitter—beginning when she was fourteen.

Aspen Ski Patrol had previously asked the Kennedys to stop playing their dangerous game. Characteristic of their lenient approach to celebrity recklessness, however, they did not yank their lift tickets. In fact, according to one report, a member of the ski patrol was part of it.

The Kennedys have been attracted to Aspen like moths to a flame. Jackie Kennedy, a good skier who always cut an elegant figure on the slopes, frequently vacationed in Aspen with her children beginning in the '60s. Her son, John Jr., was a regular in Aspen until his death piloting a small airplane in 1999. They usually stayed at the same hotel. The story is told of one-way footprints in new snow outside their third-floor hotel window to the edge of the roof, far above the heated swimming pool.

Conor Kennedy, known better for having dated Taylor Swift than being Bobby Kennedy's grandson, was arrested in a bar fight while in his early twenties. Aspen police reported that they found him "rolling around on the ground," exchanging punches with another man.

Conor's father said he was defending a friend who had been called a homophobic slur. The judge let him off with a $500 fine and a promise to stay away from alcohol and drugs for…six months. No word on whether he fulfilled his sentence, but he has not been arrested in Aspen for bar-fighting since.

Michael Kennedy's nephew, Bobby Kennedy III—the grandson of the real Bobby Kennedy—directed a fictional biopic in 2021 about Hunter Thompson called *Fear and Loathing in Aspen*. Rotten Tomatoes thought it was thoroughly rotten. A critic scathed, "You don't have to be a fan of Thompson and his work to find Fear and Loathing in Aspen a cheap, crude and woefully inadequate work that squanders a fascinating subject."

As mentioned earlier, the suicide rate in Aspen is about double the national average. Elaborate excuses are offered for this shocking level of dysfunction. Some say it's the altitude, though Sherpas in Nepal seem not to suffer the same effect. Some say it's the wealth. Some say it's because people in this small town are weirdly isolated from one another, even though they see familiar faces every day.

These contrived explanations dodge the obvious. It's the drugs.

It was drugs, including but certainly not limited to alcohol, that was the biggest and most destructive legacy of the '60s. People who came to Aspen for reasons of image are often the kind of people who abuse drugs more than others (though I am certain the Paepckes never did). Initially, they use drugs for the same reason they dress in high style, throw lavish parties, and do the other vain and foolish things they do. It is to impress the people around them and because it gives them a pleasurable physiological sensation. Later, they use drugs because they are addicted to them.

Oops.

Drugs do serve to drug you. The effect can range from a mild high to violence, delusions, hallucinations, insanity, distraction, laziness, withdrawal, stupor, comas, imprisonment, death, and—yikes!—poverty.

None of these effects comports with mainstream human function. With a high population of drug users, Aspen thus became an outlier of humanity. Aspen got messed up and attracted a lot of people who were similarly messed up.

Take Ted Bundy. He was not a resident of Aspen but was just passing through in 1974 with some time to kill. He raped, bludgeoned to death, and left in a ditch for bear food a vacationing twenty-three-year-old nurse. Bundy confessed to the crime before he was executed in 1989. His victim was about the tenth or fifteenth woman he had raped and killed.

Three years after the murder, in 1977, Aspen police pieced together enough evidence to extradite Bundy from Utah, where he was serving time for kidnapping a woman. The Utah case was a rare one where he neglected to kill his victim. Once removed to Aspen, he was held in the city jail but with privileges to visit the jail library.

Predictably enough to anyone not part of Aspen law enforcement, Bundy promptly escaped through an unlocked library window and went on to kill another two dozen women. Perhaps giving a murder suspect access to an unlocked window was a warm-up for the debate years later in Aspen as to whether cell doors should be locked. Locks are cruelly confining, you see.

The day before he was executed in Florida, Bundy gave an interview in which he said he had a normal upbringing and that there was nothing unusual about his family or friends. But two addictions stood out in his adult life of horror. One was alcohol, and the other was pornography. He described himself as addicted to porn, especially the violent and degrading kind, and said alcohol removed his inhibitions about acting on his fantasies. It is not surprising that Bundy was attracted to Aspen.

So while the '60s mostly bypassed Aspen, it did unleash a cultural tsunami that misfits and freaks rode for many years, especially in Aspen, like drunks skiing backward while playing football.

Once Aspen started partying, its sybaritic counterculture took on a life of its own. It was a case of what is called allopatric evolution—when a subgroup of a species becomes isolated and evolves into a new species. Anthropologically speaking, the Galapagos Islands have nothing over the Roaring Fork Valley except more turtles.

The post-'60s wilding of Aspen was what happened in the rest of America—but more so. While the country, as a whole, remained strongly rooted in its Western cultural heritage, Aspen was more fragile. If America in the '60s was like a conventional mom and dad who occasionally got drunk and passed out, Aspen was like their thirteen-year-old kid who got into meth and never recovered.

The intellectualism of the Paepcke clan was a thin veneer. The real Aspen of the '60s was mostly a low-brow outpost of drugged dimwits living on the edge who did not know Paepcke from Plato. Even today, the average Aspenite knows nothing of the Paepckes other than that there is a park by that name on Main Street where they go to get high. If they read this book and discover that he was an intellectual Republican capitalist who loved Beethoven, they will undoubtedly want to change the name of the park.

All this decadence and irresponsibility hastened the fall of Aspen. But the death blow was a well-intentioned socioeconomic program that shifted the town's population from druggies, dimwits, and riffraff, who were bad enough, to deadbeats, who were even worse.

CHAPTER EIGHT

MAKE IT FREE, AND THEY WILL COME: SOCIALISM ON THE SLOPES

Aspen real estate started getting expensive in the '70s. Geographically, the town is just a wide spot in the Roaring Fork Valley at an altitude of nearly eight thousand feet. To the south and east lie steep, high mountains. To the north are mountains nearly as steep though not as high. The land in all three directions is almost all government-owned in the form of the White River National Forest and several wilderness areas.

Only to the northwest, down the Roaring Fork Valley, is there significant buildable land. Even in that direction, the buildable land considered proximate to Aspen goes only as far as the narrows of Snowmass Canyon. After that, you are officially Down Valley—ugh!—and you're not with the cool kids anymore. (Apologies to Kurt Russell, Goldie Hawn, and a few other well-liked notables who live in Old Snowmass, but that's a special gig.)

The escalating real estate prices in Aspen proper were a windfall to old-timers there. The historic residential area was the quaint West End, a large flat meadow just a few hundred yards from the center of town. It was mostly built in the early part of the twentieth century with cottages and modest houses. By the mid-century, those faux Victorians were run-down and dilapidated. They were purchased by ordinary people for a song in the '50s and '60s and became very valuable in the '70s and '80s.

Today, those houses are more valuable than the silver mines ever were, with prices around \$3,000–\$5,000 a square foot. Three-thousand-square-foot houses in the West End commonly sell for eight figures.

The square footage of housing is so valuable that residents routinely lift the entire house to dig a basement to add more. Sometimes the basement extends under the lawn too. Basements being basements, they have few, if any, windows. But Aspen being Aspen, the new owners did not come to town for the outdoor views. They come for the indoor ones.

Even though these basements are invisible from outside the house, their existence bugs the local antidevelopment crowd—which is to say, the mayor, all of the city council, the newspapers, Aspen Public Radio, and especially the bureaucrats in the Building Office from whom the owner has to extract a permit. Because, well, nobody should have such a big basement.

I lived in the West End myself for a few years in a 1910 Victorian. It had been owned for decades long ago by a lady who kept horses in the backyard, though the entire property was less than one-eighth of an acre. I did an extensive remodel, taking pains to update the electrical, plumbing, and mechanical systems and generally make the place more habitable and attractive while maintaining its Victorian charm.

The house had been listed on the City Historic Register, so I was severely limited in what I could do to the exterior. The front door was original, with a single-pane window and extensive cracking and splitting of the thin wooden frame. When the sun shined on the door in the afternoon, a sliver of sunlight came through the boards and onto the floor of the entryway. When the wind blew, I could feel the breeze come through the cracks. It was not only extremely energy inefficient but also obviously not up to current building codes in Aspen or anywhere else. If the function of a door is to keep the inside and outside separated, this one was not performing its function. If it had been a door to a bathroom, I'd have been arrested for indecent exposure.

I hired a skilled cabinetmaker to fabricate an identical door, but thicker and with double pane glass—a door up to code but respectful of the house and its history. From both inside and out, the new door would look exactly like the old door, minus the cracks and splits. I figured the new one would save me zillions of dollars on my heating bill and would be welcomed by my neighbors.

But the Aspen Historical Society said no. Sometimes referred to as the Aspen Hysterical Society, they said I was prohibited from replacing that door. I had no choice but to store my expensive, perfect, historically correct new door in the garage and continue to use my cheap, broken old one. All the while, another branch of local government begged other homeowners and me to take free taxpayer money from them to install eyesore solar panels. Because global warming.

Sadly, one night after the Historical Society had given its final blessing to my completed remodel, the fragile old door broke.

Maybe it was a bear trying to get in. Could have been a mere gust of wind. Before sunup, I succeeded in replacing it with the new one I'd stored in the garage.

Weeks later, I was sitting on my little front porch right outside my new door, tilting a Coors, when an ancient pickup rolled by. It paused for minutes at the stop sign at the end of the street and then backed up all the way to my house. An elderly lady cranked down the window and cried out, "Do you live here?"

I got up and walked to her truck. "Yes, I do," I replied.

"I used to live here many years ago," she explained in a scratchy voice. She started to tell me about the backyard horses.

"Would you like to see the inside of the house, ma'am?" I asked.

"Yes. Yes, I would."

I showed her all around. The old backyard/horse pasture was mostly filled with a garage built by the previous owner, which she disapproved of, but the rest she liked a lot. After we shared more Coors and she told me again about the horses, she ambled back to her truck. "You did good. You fixed up the house, but you did it in a way that honored it. Thank you for that."

I sold that house a few years later. The purchaser gutted the interior, dug a basement extending underground halfway to the street, and remade the interior with an ultramodern décor. It is now a Victorian on the outside and something like a modern downtown Miami high-rise condo on the inside. He sold it for about double what he had paid me for it.

I didn't care, but I hope my elderly friend never saw the interior.

This fix-and-flip stuff was popular in Aspen because there's very little vacant land that isn't national forest or otherwise government-owned. Some of the fix-and-flips were done quite well, and some of them were done badly. Nearly all of them were done lucratively.

It was a gold mine for the old-timers. As real estate values went up, they cashed in. They sold their houses for ten times what they'd paid for them, bought a bigger and better house in Down Valley for much less, and used the difference to fund their retirements. Not bad for old ski instructors who had saved nothing at all.

But the young ones were not as lucky. They were not around in the '50s and '60s, so they had no old house to live in or cash out of. What they had was rent, and the rent was getting too damn high.

Alternatively, they had a thirty-minute commute from Down Valley—which is about the average commute in America, except that the drive from Down Valley to Aspen is a lot prettier than, say, the Jersey Turnpike. And there is a nearly-free bus with Wi-Fi that stops at quarter-million-dollar heated stone and glass bus stops along the way.

To the gimme/takers, however, a thirty-minute commute up the Roaring Fork Valley in a luxurious bus is an extravagant amount of wasted time. They prefer spending their time and money on skiing, and so they became convinced that they deserve to.

Paradise should be affordable and within walking distance, they told themselves. If Aspen houses are affordable for hedge fund managers to enjoy as vacation homes when they are not working seventy-hour weeks on Wall Street, it's only fair that ski instructors "working" seven months a year should have the same luxury. Paradise is no paradise if it's a thirty-minute commute away or if someone else has more than you do. That's hell.

This pervasive sense of envy and entitlement spawned the Aspen affordable housing program. The usual justifications were offered for this redistribution of wealth from moneyed people to unmoneyed ones.

The true reason unmoneyed people do not have much money is, of course, that they have not done the things that people pay a lot of money for. Teaching people how to slide down snowy hills on slippery boards does not pay well, even when supplemented with generous, tax-evading cash tips.

Most people are in agreement with that. (A few believe, or at least say, that the reason moneyed people have money is that they stole it from the rest of us, but that's a small, crazy subgroup.)

Here is where the wealth redistributors diverge from the rest of us. The redistributors would say that the reason unmoneyed people have not done much to earn money is that they are not greedy, and the reason moneyed people have is that they are. Ergo, those who do not have much money are better people—less greedy—than those who do.

Aspen should be made affordable, they said, to the un-greedy, unmoneyed people because they are superior human beings to the greedy, moneyed ones.

There is more than a little irony in this bash-the-rich mentality. It is rich people like the Paepckes who built this place, and it is still the rich who fund it through enormous property taxes. Consider the property taxes paid by a Wall Street titan on his $20 million vacation home. For that, he gets the street plowed, but he uses nothing in school services—his kids are enrolled in posh

New York prep schools—and very little in police, fire, medical, or library services. In fact, he is probably in town only a few weeks a year. Yet, he not only gets soaked by the locals; he gets practically nothing in return except their vilification.

The wealth redistributors are willfully blind to that sort of introspection. What they see is what they want to see—that people they envy and therefore perceive as greedy, shallow, and materialistic get unfairly rewarded, while generous, deep, nonmaterialistic people such as themselves do not. The solution to this unfairness is obvious: Money—or at least houses—should be taken from the greedy, shallow, materialistic people who earned them and given to the generous, deep, nonmaterialistic people who did not. At the point of a gun, if necessary.

This act of taking wealth away from those who earned it—by legislation, coercion, or force—miraculously and conveniently cleanses the wealth. It is no longer evil in the hands of the takers because the takers did not engage in the evil of greedily earning it. They instead stole…er…liberated it from an evildoer who did. In short, wealth redistributors such as the leftie locals of Aspen believe money is fine, so long as it is not earned. The less you do to earn it, the less greedy you are, and therefore, the more you deserve it.

In promoting their new taxpayer-subsidized housing scheme a few decades ago, they naturally employed different rhetoric. They complained that the escalating cost of houses in Aspen was driving out the old-timers.

But old-timers were not being driven out against their will. They were voluntarily selling their houses in a windfall that funded their retirement. They were being driven out of Aspen only in the sense that winning the lottery would drive me out of my current house and car.

The only people being "driven out" of Aspen by escalating real estate prices were thus people who had never lived there to begin with—newly arrived service workers who wanted a piece of paradise but not badly enough to pay high rent or endure a thirty-minute commute. They wanted their paradise complete with a slope-side condo paid for by someone else.

That someone would have to be someone with money since housing is not free. That's perfect because, as already explained, those people are evil for having greedily earned it, so it's only right that their money be taken from them by someone who is untainted by the greedy earning of it. Such as themselves.

Greedy earning is evil; greedy stealing is economic justice. This rationale is convenient to the takers because they like stealing more than they like earning.

These new arrivals intent on promoting economic justice in the form of free housing in paradise included some cultural influencers, such as newspaper editors and reporters, television and radio hosts, and politicians.

Take Roger Marolt. He wrote a column for *The Aspen Times* for many years with a moderately leftist bent, which placed him to the extreme right of the rest of the reporters and editors until I came along to fill that slot.

Marolt is the son of a famous skier and ski coach, namely Olympian and former University of Colorado Athletic Director Bill Marolt. Though not in taxpayer-subsidized housing himself, Roger has two brothers who have lived there for many years, even though the family is not exactly impoverished. He is a fanatical proponent of the system.

After I published several columns critical of the program, the local chapter of taxpayer-subsidized radio, Aspen Public Radio, invited me to debate Marolt on the merits of it. The debate was moderated, in a manner, by the editor of the other Aspen newspaper, the *Aspen Daily News*, along with the Aspen Public Radio host. I learned after I arrived at the radio station that both these purportedly objective moderators were themselves either residents or staunch advocates of taxpayer-subsidized housing.

It was three-on-me. Words were exchanged, including some unpleasant ones after we went off-air. I don't know if I won the debate or not, but Marolt, to his credit, did apologize to me years later.

Marolt's editor at *The Aspen Times*, Rick Carroll, is another longtime beneficiary of the housing welfare program. He and his wife, who writes an opinion column for *The Aspen Times*, have a taxpayer-subsidized place in downtown Aspen that is worth several million dollars. Public records show they paid $293,000 for it.

Other beneficiaries of the program include the local politicos and bureaucrats who run the town. The longtime head of the program was himself a beneficiary of it. The chair of the Pitkin County Commissioners, Patti Clapper, has been on the housing dole for the last thirty-five years. At one time, the mayor and four of the five city council members were in taxpayer-subsidized housing.

That mayor was Michael Ireland, universally called "Mick." Raised in a prosperous Chicago family, after spending eleven years getting a psychology degree, Mick moved to Aspen to be a dishwasher and bus driver in the late '70s. Like many other

Aspenites who came from elsewhere, he likes to boast that he is a local because he has lived in Aspen longer than the person he's arguing with—as if that point wins the argument.

He has been in and out of Aspen and Pitkin County politics for over forty years while running a small-time tax practice that he effectively fed with his political connections and influence. Naturally, he also had a stint as an *Aspen Times* reporter.

Mick was appointed to fill a vacancy on the Pitkin County Commission and was subsequently elected for three additional terms. As a commissioner, he pushed relentlessly to dam tiny Castle Creek outside of town—a creek so small you can literally step across it—to build a hydroelectric plant. It was a quixotic proposal, especially coming from this psychology major. The people of Aspen ultimately voted it down.

Mick's biggest role as a county commissioner was tormenting developers. No project was too small for his meddling. After his long tenure with the Pitkin County Commission, he continued his antibusiness crusade through three terms as mayor of Aspen. He told a fawning interviewer, "This is like a calling, like someone who climbs Mount Everest."

My first exposure to Mick was when I attended a city council public meeting soon after moving to Aspen. At the outset of each meeting, the council would allow public comments. An elderly man rose and limped to the podium, rolling a wheeled oxygen bottle behind him. He started speaking with some difficulty about a parking issue near his small downtown place. Mick repeatedly interrupted him, berated him, cut him off, and was a colossal jerk to the man.

I learned later that this was typical behavior by Mick—his rudeness embarrassed even his supporters—but at the time, I was stunned. I had lived in Aspen only a few months, but I wish to this day that I had stood up and told Mick to stand down—at which time, I imagine Mick would have interrupted me to ask how long I had lived in Aspen.

My second encounter with Mick was on Facebook. My column had been published bimonthly for some time by *The Aspen Times*, and Mick took exception to it. He posted it on his own Facebook page with the comment, "Aspen, it's not for everyone. Maybe you should move on." Mick was my mayor at the time.

A few years later, Mick infamously crashed a private party in a local park, ate their food and drink, and cursed a woman attendee. When an eighty-four-year-old man asked Mick to leave, Mick took a swing at him. Apparently hoping to get ahead of the breaking news of his behavior, Mick promptly went home and posted on Facebook a story contradicted by several eyewitnesses—he claimed he had been assaulted in the park.

Another crash by Mick ended even worse for him. He is an avid bicyclist and often posts pictures of himself on social media in bicycling spandex. One day, he was coasting down steep Independence Pass. Gravity was his friend. Perhaps they were lovers, because he was going pretty fast.

Then gravity betrayed him. Recall that he was not a physics major. He had draped his bike lock over his handlebars. Aided by the bouncing of his bike over the rough pavement, gravity pulled the lock off the handlebars and into the spokes of his front wheel.

Gravity was not done with him. As the lock tangled with the spokes and bicycle frame, the wheel seized up and stopped spinning. Since things in motion tend to stay in motion, when the bike stopped, Mick didn't. He cartwheeled over the handlebars at an impressive altitude and velocity.

He lived, but his political life soon died for unrelated reasons. He was term-limited out of the mayor's office. Before that happened, however, he schemed with another city councilman to switch seats. Mick would take the city council position while the existing city councilman took the mayor position—but with Mick behind the throne. That was too much even for Aspen, and their scheme was shot down.

Mick ran for city council anyway. He was universally endorsed by both newspapers and the rest of the liberal Aspen establishment. But his abrasive personality, party-crashing, mild sociopathy, tight spandex, concussed head, and seat-switching scheme added up to a trouncing this time. He also was not helped by the yard signs sprouting up around town printed "Sick of Mick." He should be glad that the rhyme was not worse.

He still was not done, however. He ran for tax assessor for Pitkin County. He wanted to be the guy deciding how much the rich folks got taxed, and it would be a lot. "How much is my tax this year?" would be answered with "How much ya got?" Again, he was crushed in the election, that time, by an unknown newcomer. It was not because Aspen liked the newcomer or suddenly developed a dislike for taxing the rich. It was because they were sick of Mick. In my column, I could not resist suggesting, "Aspen, it's not for everyone. Maybe you should move on."

But he has not. Most recently and perhaps predictably, Mick's tax practice has morphed into a consulting practice, where he sells his city connections to the developers he used to excoriate.

(The current mayor is named Torre. That one word is literally his whole legal name, and it might be one more than he has earned. He and the city council spend the town's quarter-billion-dollar annual budget, which amounts to over $30,000 per Aspenite. His qualification for the job of mayor is that he was a tennis instructor—and, of course, a staunch advocate for more taxpayer-subsidized housing.)

Mick has not run or even bicycled for anything lately. But he still writes a column for a local newspaper, name-calls people he disagrees with politically, crashes parties, and enjoys the multimillion-dollar digs he has been living in for thirty years at taxpayer expense.

Mick purchased his multimillion-dollar place for $91,000. His sister is on the housing dole too. She bought hers for $158,000. So are many of Mick's other friends and cronies. All this happened while he was a county commissioner and then mayor, making administrative, managerial, and financial decisions, including whether to gift city money to the underfunded HOAs. Not once did he recuse himself for having a conflict of interest.

Mick and his friends have successfully assembled and launched this taxpayer-subsidized housing scheme into an enormous, untouchable entitlement program. Administered as the "Aspen Pitkin County Housing Authority" or APCHA, they have over three thousand units in inventory. Those units are collectively worth well over $3,000,000,000. Yes, $3 billion—with a *b*.

Do the math. That works out to over a million dollars per unit. Residents pay dimes on the dollar for them. Many are slopeside and worth several times that. These are not exactly the projects in Chicago.

Although the program supposedly encourages "diversity" in Aspen, hardly any of the residents of the projects are people of color. Nearly all are older, upper-middle-class, liberal white people.

I lived for five years at the top of Mill Street, a very nice, small neighborhood a few hundred feet above town. It is higher in elevation than the lift and gondola serving the mountain, so I skied *down* from my house to get to the lift. Next door was a quadplex of taxpayer-subsidized units that were closer to the slope than I was. These units have a true market value upward of $5 million each. According to public records, the residents paid less than $300,000.

The money for this program comes from taxing the rich. Aspen City Council in 1990 imposed a 1 percent tax on the sale of residential real estate. That is in addition to the 0.5 percent tax for the Wheeler Opera House, discussed earlier. Both taxes are paid by the buyer, but of course, they lessen the proceeds to the seller by the amount of them, just as any other sales tax does.

At Aspen real estate prices, this 1 percent tax for housing welfare generates a lot of revenue. It generated well over $20 million last year alone in a real estate market with gross sales volumes of over $2 billion. The city skims off administration costs—the salaries and offices of APCHA add up to a couple million—and uses the rest to buy and build new housing. Being government types, their business acumen is not great. They typically buy and build at the height of the real estate cycle. When they sell, which is not often, it is typically at the market troughs.

Aspen enacted this tax just before Colorado passed an amendment to the state constitution in 1992 prohibiting new taxes without citizen approval. Today's APCHA housing residents would probably approve even a 5 percent real estate transfer tax—maybe to pay for Club Med facilities at their buildings—since they personally would pay hardly any of it. But it is not certain that the 1995 residents would have approved even the 1 percent.

The most recent subsidized housing boondoggle is a 277-unit project at the old lumberyard a few miles from downtown. It is projected to cost $425 million, which works out to over $1.5 million per unit.

Even more shocking is the cost per citizen of Aspen. With something over seven thousand citizens, it comes to a charge of $55,000 per citizen or around $100,000 per household just for this one project. The total market value of Aspen's subsidized housing—over $3 million—divided by the seven thousand total citizens of the city comes out to about a half million per citizen.

For a fraction of the money sitting in its subsidized housing, Aspen could build much of the pipe-dream monorail it fantasizes about to connect with Down Valley.

The Micks have an answer to critics who complain that this giveaway is too expensive. They say free housing for them is not so much for them but for the rest of us. We give millions to the Micks so that we can be graced with more Micks. They make this argument with a straight face.

Who needs another Walter Paepcke remaking Aspen into Athens when Mick can remake it into a clown circus by riding around in spandex so he can take swings at eighty-four-year-old men and curse ladies in the park while stealing their food?

To become a resident of the taxpayer-subsidized housing program, there are two financial requirements. First, the most recent tax return of the resident-to-be cannot show over $212,000 in annual income for a couple. (This figure is as of Jan. 1, 2022; the threshold is lower for a single and higher for a household.) Of course, their tax returns will not show unreported income, such as tips to servers, ski instructors, and the like. Once the resident is in a unit, the resident's income can go up as much as 50 percent. That upward-revised limit brings the income limit for a couple to over $300,000.

Second, the couple's net assets cannot exceed $984,000—they can nearly be millionaires. Moreover, no attempt is made to verify the net worth number they provide. It is whatever number they report to APCHA. The reported number is under penalty of criminal perjury, but there has never been a prosecution for perjurious numbers.

These residents are well-to-do passengers on a housing welfare gravy train, not society's misfortunates. Aspen hardly has any misfortunates, wealth-wise. One that hung around half a dozen years ago was called "the homeless guy." He eventually moved on. His departure did not stop the town from applying for and receiving half a million dollars in COVID-19 money intended to serve the homeless.

There is a homeless shelter in town run by a dedicated longtime citizen with some sense, Vince Savage. Pitkin County officialdom agitated for a while about building a much bigger shelter, but Savage warned that more free services would attract more people seeking them. APCHA could learn a thing or two from Savage.

APCHA residents are also supposed to work at least 1,500 hours a year in Pitkin County and are not supposed to own other real estate in the county. As with the net worth limit, little attempt is made to periodically confirm that status. And again, no one has ever been prosecuted for lying.

In addition, the work requirement is waived once a person is in the unit and decides to retire. Retirees seldom move out because there is no better housing deal on earth. As a result, this program, originally intended to house local workers, has skewed wildly over the years toward old retirees. The average age of residents is now in the mid-fifties. Some 23 percent are over sixty-five. Some have not worked for decades. Meanwhile, many are now in multiple-bedroom units even after their husband, wife, significant other, or kids have moved out. Once a resident is in, they get to stay when the size and composition of their household change. It is not rare for an empty nester couple or an individual to have a two- or three-bedroom place.

Moves to shift this housing intended for workers back to workers are shouted down by the nonworker residents of the housing. A recent letter to *The Aspen Times* asked rhetorically (if ungrammatically), "What is someone supposed to do if they want to live here, but doesn't work here, can't afford free market rent, and are not allowed in taxpayer-subsidized housing?"

Good question. One might also wonder, "What is someone supposed to do if they want a Bentley, but doesn't have a job, can't afford one, and are not given a free one by the taxpayers?"

Another reason retirees do not leave is that, in a sense, they are trapped there. If they were to sell, their sale price is limited by APCHA to the extremely discounted price they paid years ago plus a 3 percent per year inflation escalator. That 3 percent per year is not bad as a guaranteed return, especially when the owner lived rent-free in million-dollar digs for years, but it is not what they could have gotten in Aspen for free-market real estate.

Being trapped in nearly-free lodging in paradise is OK with most of the residents, but a significant number want an even sweeter deal. After buying their places for dimes on the dollar, largely at taxpayer expense, and living in them nearly free for decades, they want to be allowed to sell them for dollars on the dollar—at market prices. Their argument for that approach is that they want the money. And they deserve the money because—as mentioned—they're not greedy like those who earn it.

The effect would be a monstrous giveaway of millions of dollars to each resident—after the resident has already enjoyed subsidized housing for decades. But at least it would kill the program.

Demand for this honey/money trap exceeds supply and, of course, always will. Who would not want to live in a multimillion-dollar place alongside the Aspen ski slopes for dimes on the dollar? As a result, units become available only when the resident dies—since no one moves out except horizontally—or when the city builds or buys more units.

Newly available units are assigned to new residents through periodic lotteries. Aspen insiders seem to win lots of the lotteries, and sometimes, they are allowed to bypass the lottery altogether. One such insider was a city employee who bypassed the lottery on the grounds of disability. The disability was that his wife got migraines.

One of the rules of APCHA is that residents are not allowed to rent out their units because such rentals undercut the justification for the program to provide local housing for local workers. But this rule has been honored mainly in the breach. Residents commonly rent out their million-dollar units for thousands of dollars a night over Christmas week or other popular times and use the proceeds for their own vacations and supplemental income. Many even shamelessly list their units on vacation home rental sites like Airbnb or VRBO, usually with impunity.

Their rental income is seldom reported on their tax returns because reporting it would cost them taxes and would be visible to APCHA (at least if APCHA ever doublechecked such things).

The longtime administrator of APCHA, himself an APCHA resident and a crony of Mick Ireland, was blind to violations. He finally retired while continuing to live in his unit and was replaced by a young reformer who tried to clean things up. The reformer was fired in about three years.

The result of all this is that illicit and unreported income, together with ongoing violations of the income and net worth limits in APCHA, has made a sizable portion of Aspen residents into APCHA violators, perjurers, and criminal tax cheats.

The politicians making the decisions as to whether to fix the program are residents of the program themselves or are cronies of residents. They don't want to fix it. For them, it works great. Repeated calls for an audit of the program are fiercely shot down. These taxpayer-subsidized residences are henhouses chock full of foxes.

I often wrote in my *Aspen Times* column about the taxpayer-subsidized crime spree. But nothing ever happened other than the editors at the newspaper living in APCHA housing got jittery. One day, a television investigative reporter from Denver came to Aspen with a camera crew to interview me. I told him the sordid story, he was outraged, and we made the nightly news in Denver.

But again, nothing happened except that my windshield got smashed at the grocery store in broad daylight.

This whole criminal enterprise should be the subject of a RICO investigation by the US Attorneys' Office. But that has not happened yet because these APCHA residents/reprobates carry a lot of political clout. The entire population of Aspen is only about 7,200 people, and half of them live in APCHA housing. Local politicians are about as likely to mess with the APCHA entitlement as national politicians are likely to mess with Social Security.

The APCHA projects typically are governed by a homeowners' association, much like ordinary free-market condominium complexes. The HOA is an elected body of building residents charged with collecting dues and maintaining the structure. In theory, anyway. In practice, the buildings are in miserable repair and are burdened with millions in outstanding deferred maintenance because the residents are not willing to pay sufficient HOA dues to maintain them. HOA reserves for the projects are 78 percent underfunded. Some buildings are now barely habitable and could be condemned for safety reasons, except that the safety inspectors—many of whom live in the units or have friends who do—look the other way.

The buildings are falling apart for three reasons. The first is that the residents have little incentive to maintain their buildings in good repair because the resale price if they sold them is fixed by APCHA. Capital improvements to the common spaces are unrecoverable. Their resale price is $XX.XX whether the roof leaks or not.

The second reason is that the city frequently considers subsidizing the HOAs with taxpayer money—as if the initial subsidy of purchasing or building the units and then selling them to the residents for dimes on the dollar was not enough of a giveaway. Why should the residents pay to maintain the buildings if the city is likely to do it for free if they don't?

The third reason is that many of the residents are just those sorts of people (not all—a few are friends of mine). Those sorts of people believe they are entitled to freebies. Free housing is one of their freebies. Free maintenance of that housing is another. Free and untaxed rental income from illegally renting out their APCHA unit over Christmas week for $10,000 is another.

The genius of their life of freebies is that they simultaneously convince themselves they are morally superior to the people paying for their freebies because those people were greedy workaholics in earning the money that the freeloaders kindly relieve them of. Their refrain reduces to, "You're greedy and I'm not, so I'm going to take your money! Gimme!"

Such people tend to be of a particular political persuasion. They tend to be hard-left. They tend to be sanctimonious, atheistic, lazy, pleasure-seeking, egotistical, spandex-wearing, self-centered, generous-with-other-people's-money, power-hungry hypocrites. They tend to be Mick Ireland.

In the taxpayer-subsidized housing game, Mick gets around. After the people expelled him from elected office, he wormed his way back into a position of power in the scheme. He got his politician and bureaucrat friends to hire him as the APCHA "Hearing Officer" for $150/hour. In that job, he makes quasi-judicial judgments as to which people qualify for the subsidized housing and which don't.

He has already been formally charged in court filings with bias and conflicts of interest by a couple who complained that Mick was "prosecutorial," "repeatedly disrespectful," "biased," riddled with "many conflicts of interest" and not "fair and impartial." *The Aspen Times* whitewashed the matter in an article by the aforementioned reporter and editor Rick Carroll who happens to be a resident of the projects and a pal of Mick.

Ironically, these advocates of and participants in free taxpayer-subsidized housing oppose any new development in Aspen that might alleviate the housing crunch simply because they are reflexively antidevelopment—because they are reflexively anti-business.

The effect of this antidevelopment sentiment is to prevent any increase in the supply of housing. The local lefties are willing to deny their constituents the housing product they desire if that is what's necessary to deny the businesses that provide that product the profits they would make by providing it. The lefties' purported love for people is exceeded by their hatred for businesses that make a profit by serving those people.

The city council once granted approval for a renovation of a downtown building conditioned on the developer leasing the basement to an "affordable" restaurant. The city would set the menu and prices at this city-regulated affordable restaurant. I ran a contest in my column for readers to name the proposed government-regulated restaurant. The winner for the restaurant name was "Castro's Corner," and the winner for a menu item was "Pol Pot Pie."

The space sat empty for years. The restaurant business is hard enough without the government dictating menus and prices. The city finally waived the restriction.

The predictable outcome of the city's heavy-handed attempt to make Aspen restaurants affordable was consequently to delay for years the opening of one. Meanwhile, existing restaurants quietly applauded the city's price and menu diktats that delayed the proposed competition to them.

The city has also proposed banning new franchise and chain store retailers. They seem to think that places like Recreational Equipment, Inc., P. F. Chang's, The Gap, and other chains are evil. They adversely affect the local economy because customers like them.

When it was pointed out that this ban would close the main grocery store—owned by Kroger—along with Ace Hardware and other businesses that locals not only like but need, including the local gas station, they modified the proposal so as to grandfather in existing chains. No reason was offered for why existing chains are good but new ones are bad. The reason is apparently that people would miss the existing ones if they disappeared but would not miss the new ones because they don't know what they're missing.

If Vail Resorts were to buy SkiCo, as they have bought many other resorts, the city's ban would apparently ban SkiCo and thereby close the ski mountain.

There was one McDonald's in town for a long time. It was just two blocks from the gondola. Locals liked it, but it eventually closed. There was much mourning by a city council lacking the self-awareness to realize that they had recently prohibited anything similar from taking its place.

There are two notable exceptions to the official Aspen hostility to business. The first is the Mick exception. Mick does not oppose developments so long as the developer hires him for "consulting" services.

The second exception is that officialdom invariably supports new developments if the development is for taxpayer-subsidized housing. As mentioned, the demand for houses in paradise for dimes on the dollar exceeds supply and always will. Build more, and if you make it nearly free, they will come. And they do.

The result is that the partisan lefties on one hand shrilly oppose any further development of Aspen and any further population increase in the town. And on the other hand, they simultaneously and stridently advocate for additional taxpayer-subsidized housing developments to attract more people—people like themselves, who not only want to live in paradise but want to live there for free. Because equity.

Their advocacy for additional buildings for taxpayer-subsidized housing is so single-minded that they commonly waive ordinary building codes to permit the building of such places. Things like setbacks, density limitations, height, bulk, and other matters of safety and aesthetics are enforced fanatically against ordinary builders, not so much for safety or aesthetic reasons but simply to get in the way of development. But they are routinely waived when it comes to taxpayer-subsidized housing.

They will also waive such regulations for ordinary builders, but only if the builder ponies up some moolah for the taxpayer-subsidized housing program. The builder is put in the position of bribing the city to get the permits he is obligated to get and entitled to receive.

The mayor and city council never met a taxpayer-subsidized housing project they didn't like, just as they never met a non-taxpayer-subsidized housing project that they did—unless they were paid to.

Here is what should be done to fix the taxpayer-subsidized housing system in Aspen, short of just ending the program and letting market forces produce the needed housing—a pill that Aspenites would never swallow since half of them are on the housing dole.

First, it is important that the units be rented to residents, not sold to them. This is for several good reasons. When they own them, they ironically have no incentive to maintain them because their resale prices are limited to what they paid for them—dimes on the dollar—plus a modest inflation adjustment. Owners have little incentive to fix the roof because the cost of fixing the roof is not recoverable in the sale of their unit.

It is also easier to evict renters than owners, and many residents deserve eviction. Many violate the prohibitions on renting out their units for holiday windfalls. Many are lousy neighbors. Many are in violation of the income and wealth limits.

The legal scenario for the system is more consistent with a leasehold than a property deed anyway. The property deed in the current ownership system is "restricted," so the owner cannot simply sell his unit unencumbered at fair market value or modify it or legally rent it out. It is called a deed, but the restrictions in the deed make it much more like a leasehold.

Once the system is converted into rental units rather than deed-restricted ownership, the restrictions should be vigorously enforced against the owners.

But one restriction should be relaxed a bit. That is the restriction on re-renting the units on a short-term basis. An economist would say that it is economically inefficient for a renter to go on vacation for a week or a month and not be allowed to rent out his residence. In a town where the politicos agitate for inexpensive vacation accommodations, it is paradoxical that residents of taxpayer-subsidized housing are not allowed to provide short-term rentals to vacationers.

But consideration should be given to the fact that the place being rented out is owned by the taxpayer, not the renter. In view of that, the resident should share the rental proceeds with the taxpayers. Split the rent 50/50. Let the renter keep 50 percent of the proceeds to compensate him for his effort in arranging the rental and his loss of the unit for the duration of the rental. Give the other 50 percent to the taxpayers, in recognition that the unit is owned by them.

Finally, limit short-term re-rentals to a total of thirty days a year. The primary purpose of the taxpayer-subsidized housing program is to provide housing for qualified locals, after all, not to get those locals into the landlord business by permitting them to rent out housing owned by taxpayers.

Allowing short-term re-rentals where half the rental income comes back to the taxpayers would single-handedly generate millions in new revenue for the system, millions in income for the residents, and thousands of inexpensive unit-nights for visitors.

Next, tighten the income and wealth limitations. It is absurd that taxpayer-subsidized housing is given to a couple making over $300,000 a year with a net worth of nearly a million dollars. The income limit should be more like $150,000 a year for a couple, with a net worth limitation of $300,000. The residents should lose privileges if their income or wealth exceeds the limit for two straight years.

Get the oldsters out. People over fifty-five no longer working in the county should lose this taxpayer subsidy that was established for workers. A new, younger worker should take their place in the workforce and in taxpayer-subsidized housing. This is supposed to be a worker housing program, not a taxpayer-funded retirement home.

The program should be scaled back. It will never be big enough to meet demand because billions of people in the world would like a piece of it. Decide how big it really needs to be, and limit it to that. The local politicos are not willing to do this because it would require them to admit that their goal is not a number; it's just "more."

In establishing the size of the program, policy makers should bear in mind that it is local businesses that should be primarily responsible for compensating employees in a manner that enables them to attract those employees. That is how it's done in the real world. Employers pay their workers what is necessary to attract and keep them, which naturally takes into account their housing costs. It should not be the responsibility of taxpayers to pick up part of businesses' employee costs by paying for the employees' housing so that the businesses can pay the employees less.

Some businesses have been taking advantage of this for years. None is worse than SkiCo, which incessantly lobbies for more taxpayer money to be spent on more housing for their workers. Their lobbying is all couched in sanctimony, as if they are looking out for the good of Aspen and its workers.

The truth is exactly the opposite. SkiCo lobbies for more taxpayer money to be spent on subsidized housing for a purely selfish financial reason. It is so that they can keep worker wages low. The effect is that the taxpayer subsidy goes to SkiCo. Rather than paying their workers a wage to enable them to live in the vicinity or providing worker housing as part of their compensation, they pay them peanuts while dangling the possibility of winning the taxpayer-subsidized housing lottery. Maybe the workers will win Powerball too.

In this and other political issues, SkiCo has elevated selfish lobbying to a hypocritical and sanctimonious art form. Consider global warming, next up.

CHAPTER NINE

GLOBAL WARMING ENDS WORLD: BLACK AND GAY SKIERS HARDEST HIT

If SkiCo did not have global warming to worry about, it would have to invent it. You cannot ride a chair lift or buy a ski pass or visit their website without being bombarded by news of the impending skiing holocaust. You should worry—a lot! But know that SkiCo is there to save us. You should thank them while you're shelling out twenty-three dollars for a hamburger in an on-slope restaurant.

Meanwhile, consider yourself lucky that the past parade of horrible predictions that global warming would end the world by now has proven, well, horrible. But don't get cocky because that would make you a "denier."

"Denier" is the epithet hurled by the global warming doomsayers at anyone who questions the accuracy of their past predictions that the world would be ended by now. The arctic was predicted to be ice-free a decade ago. I deny the accuracy of that prediction. Snow was predicted to be extinct years ago. I deny the accuracy of that prediction too. Barack Obama's beach mansion was predicted to be underwater even before he bought it. I deny the accuracy of that prediction, much as I wish it were true. Denying the accuracy of those predictions merely because they proved inaccurate makes me a "denier."

There's still time left for the world to end, granted, but we are noticeably off-track from the predicted countdown.

The accuracy of the new global warming fanatics is about the same as the accuracy of the old religious ones. Indeed, the two groups have a lot in common. Both are fervent and faithful in their convictions. Both see their predictions as a righteous damning of flawed and fallen humankind. Both curse the unbelievers. Both seem to take a perverse delight in their dire predictions and actively pray for them to come true.

Before you sentence me to mild discomfort in the warmth of hell, know that I am not really a denier when it comes to global warming. It's just that I'm not religious about it, either.

It does look like the earth's temperature has increased a couple of degrees in the last few hundred years, but it's hard to say how much of that is human-caused—hence reversible by human actions. We are certainly putting a lot of carbon into the atmosphere, which, in simple computer models, produces a warm greenhouse effect, but the earth is not simple at all. For example, more warmth can be self-correcting to some extent by increasing oceanic evaporation, which produces more cloud cover.

Moreover, it is hard to say whether a slightly warmer earth is a good or bad thing. It's a fact that temperatures on earth were warmer for most of its history than they are now. During that warm history, plant, animal, and human life evolved. Chemical reactions—including biochemical ones—typically are facilitated at warmer temperatures where molecules are more active. That is why humans and other mammals are warm-blooded.

Polar ice caps are not the norm for the earth. Geologically speaking, we are now at an interstice in ice ages. Ice ages are rough on life. Both plant and animal biomass plummet. Any knowledgeable botanist would say a drop of three degrees in earth temperatures would be catastrophic to crop yields and result in widespread starvation. If you think a warm day in Seattle is inconvenient, you should see what happens to wheat prices when Nebraska is covered by glaciers.

As for weather events, it's journalists and leftist politicians, not scientists, who say we have more hurricanes, tornados, and wildfires than we used to. On this matter of science, I'll trust the scientists.

That said, we should certainly practice conservation. It is the prudent and right thing to do. We should not use more of the earth's resources than is reasonably necessary. Future generations may need those resources. Even if they don't, the thrifty Scot in me abhors waste. Regular readers know that I have a thing against monster pickup trucks, especially the tailgating kind, and that I do a lot of walking. Tread lightly.

For all their anti-capitalist rhetoric, Warmingites don't tread lightly at all. They are ideologues, not conservationists. That's why they won't embrace nuclear energy, which is carbon-free. They don't want to solve the problem they've conjured up; they want to milk it.

The motivation of the Left is generally not to solve problems but to use them, mostly to make them feel good about themselves.

They want to feel morally superior to those who disagree with them. Righteous sanctimony feels good, as the old-time religious end-of-worlders knew well. That is why leftists make a show of their moral superiority with silly preening, such as platitude-filled yard signs or COEXIST bumper stickers—which, it should be noted, cost them nothing beyond the price of the sign or sticker.

Once the Warmingites deem the deniers inferior, they are happy not to solve the problem that the deniers deny. The deniers made their bed hot; now, they can roast in it. Warmingites think it is only right that the world they share with these inferior deniers should end. The Warmingites hate humanity for being a bunch of deplorables or, in the new vernacular, a bunch of semi-fascists and ultra-MAGAs.

Whatever their name for people who analyze evidence rather than faithfully following failing predictions, the Warmingites truly think of humanity as a cancer on the earth, a sacrilege against their nature gods, a blasphemy against Gaia. They are willing to go down with the ship so long as the ship does go down. That martyrdom, too, makes them feel superior. If the end of humanity entails the end of them, it's worth it because the world will be a better place without us. Never mind the question: Better by what measure, in a world with no aesthete capable of making the measurement?

Back to the warming warnings of our moral superiors at SkiCo. Oceans will rise catastrophically and then probably boil away. Droughts will be common. Wine grapes will shrivel up, and we'll have to drink the screw-cap kind or maybe even box wine. Water will turn to blood. Locusts. Lice. Frogs. Deniers. Trumpsters. Ultra-MAGAs. Worst of all, SkiCo warns, skiing will be lousy because there will be no snow. It will be even worse than the drought winter of '76–'77.

A spoof *New York Times* headline was made famous by Rush Limbaugh years ago:

"World Ends: Women and Minorities Hardest Hit"

The point of the spoof was that the *New York Times* and other liberal media have a habit of focusing on certain demographics when reporting natural or manmade disasters that impact everyone. That's because they are eager to present the bad luck of only the demographics they feel sorry for so that you will too. Feeling sorry for people who vote for them is part of the Left's shtick.

SkiCo managed to one-up *The Aspen Times*. The demographics that SkiCo pities most are itself and its customers. The end of the world, SkiCo cries, would hit skiers—and companies like SkiCo—the hardest. You should join SkiCo in feeling pity for them and their rich customers, you should admire their courageous self-pity, and you should buy a few more twenty-five-dollar hamburgers before you jet back to your air-conditioned home in suburban Atlanta.

When you are not pitying them, SkiCo wants to enthrall you with their heroic efforts to save their customers and themselves. For example, if you have been anywhere near Aspen or SkiCo's website, you know that a couple of their ski patrol huts are powered by solar panels.

They don't mention that their whole business is to entice hundreds of thousands of people from around the world into hopping onto jets powered by petroleum-based fuel (preferably the inefficient private kind that carry spendy types) for the purpose of paying big bucks to be ferried up snowy slopes by lifts powered by electricity (generated somewhere else like Down Valley) in order to slide back down on wooden boards and then maybe get lucky downtown with a MILF plastic surgery victim.

It's all false marketing. Like medieval church patrons purchasing indulgences, SkiCo thinks a solar panel on a ski patrol hut buys salvation from the damnation of the Warmingites and their angry weather gods. It seems to work. No strangers to hypocrisy themselves, the Warmingites do go easy on SkiCo.

This sanctimony that SkiCo perfected in the global warming game is good enough to use elsewhere.

Take Black skiers.

To their acute embarrassment, SkiCo has not attracted enough Black skiers. In fact, to my knowledge, no Black person lives in Aspen at all. The nearest one is a friend of mine in Down Valley. For whatever reason—and it may be racist to say it, but I will anyway—it is a fact that Blacks don't ski much in Aspen or anywhere else. That, SkiCo decided, is a problem needing a solution, or is at least a problem needing some virtue signaling.

The head of SkiCo is Mike Kaplan, a Democrat donor rich in both money and irony. He's impeccably woke. A few years ago, he secured the hosting of the "National Brotherhood of Skiers," which advertises itself as "the largest Black ski group in the United States."

Kaplan worried, however, that SkiCo employees might be racist to the Black skiers he enticed to Aspen. A Jim Crow–style lynching would be nearly as bad for business as lower profits. To avoid that, he sent around a memo to all one thousand SkiCo employees telling them how to behave around Black people.

He led by instructing his employees to greet the Black guests "lovingly and intentionally." In other words, do not greet them accidentally or hatefully. Accidentally permitting them to hear you mutter, "I just hate Black skiers," would be bad for business.

That seems like good advice, but probably not necessary in modern America. Kaplan acknowledged that SkiCo employees ordinarily treat all guests "lovingly and intentionally" (which has always been my personal experience) but instructed them "to make an even greater effort" with the Black ones.

I suppose "Black Skiers Matter" signs will soon be popping up on Aspen's slopes. Kaplan will then have to announce that slogans such as "*All* Skiers Matter" are racist. He will have to withdraw his acknowledgment to employees that they have always treated all skiers as if they matter because, in point of woke fact, only the Black ones do. He will have to apologize for having said that all skiers matter and maybe attend diversity training, too—a fate worse than having one's lift ticket yanked.

The reason for this special effort for Blacks, Kaplan explained, is that "standard or even slightly bad service can easily be interpreted as bias." Employees should avoid saying things to customers who are Black that might be interpreted as racist, such as "that parking spot is just for hotel guests" or "you can't park there" or "my restaurant isn't open now, come back at 5." (These are actual quotes from Kaplan's memo.)

Kaplan informed employees that he knows of the hurt such rules can inflict on customers who are Black because he has talked with "friends who are Black." He must have been slumming Down Valley.

Kaplan should be given the credit he solicits for having any Black friends at all. But I think he made up the part about their feeling racially discriminated against when told that a restaurant is closed or parking is restricted.

He sums up with, "In a sense, I'm asking you to see color, to both celebrate our visitors and to recognize their lived experience, not to be color blind."

In case you are wondering, "lived" experiences are the kind liberals have.

Let's parse this. First, the implicit premise of Kaplan's memo is that he thinks SkiCo employees need this kind of guidance. He thinks that unless they are reminded to be welcoming to skiers who are Black, they're liable not to be. He apparently does not think much of his employees.

Second, isn't the color of your customers' skin less important than the contents of their wallets? Why should some customers get treated better based on their skin color? What have white, Asian, Hispanic, Native American, and skiers of other colors done to deserve worse treatment than Black skiers?

Finally, consider how Kaplan's admonition to his employees would play out. Suppose you are the valet parking attendant at a swanky hotel in Aspen. Are you supposed to let people park their cars illegally but only if they are Black?

Suppose you run a restaurant that opens at 5:00 p.m. If a couple who happens to be Black knocks on the locked door at 4:00 p.m., are you supposed to let them in and scramble to cook them dinner and serve them while the restaurant is closed and the staff has not yet arrived? What do you do if a mixed-race couple knocks on the door at 4:00 p.m.? Do you open early at 4:30 p.m.? If an individual is three-quarters Black, do you open at 4:15 p.m.?

If a white couple happens to arrive at 4:00 p.m. at the same time as the Black couple, do you let in the Black couple but not the white couple? If so, do you follow Kaplan's lead by making a big show of your racial discrimination in order to display your antiracism, or do you do it on the sly the way Harvard does?

What other rules are suspended for Blacks beyond the parking and restaurant rules? Can they rope-duck into closed slopes? Can they cut lift lines? Can they shoplift? Can they speed down Main Street drunk? Can they blow cocaine, beat up their girlfriend, and shoot their boyfriend? Would Charlie Sheen and Claudine Longet get even lighter sentences if they were Black?

It will be interesting to see how far the proud boys at SkiCo go with their boastful, self-righteous racial discrimination. I can imagine Aspen's lift ticket prices being reset in proportion to pallor. They will have a light sensor to make the measurement. A whole scam will evolve, with white guys putting on blackface to get the discounted fare—along with free parking, private dining in restaurants after hours, and lift-line cutting.

Then there was the time Kaplan or his lackeys writing under his name played the race card in an op-ed for a leading newspaper back in 2017.

His op-ed implied that then-President Trump was racist for clamping down on illegal immigrants coming over the Mexican border. The result of this racist clamp-down, Kaplan lamented, was a drop in skier visits to Aspen by rich, passport-holding Mexicans. That meant lower profits at SkiCo—as if there are a lot of rich Mexican skiers and as if they give a hoot about poor illegal immigrants.

In this two-step from an allegation of immoral racism on the part of the president to a lament that SkiCo's profits were suffering as a result, Kaplan showed his real cards. Those real cards were not moral ones but financial ones.

But he played even his financial cards from the bottom of the deck. His real concern was not that SkiCo's profits were down because of the missing rich Mexicans but because of the missing poor ones. Limiting the flow of illegals limited the pool of low-paid undocumented workers in the valley for janitorial and other menial labor. SkiCo was, therefore, faced with having to hire higher-priced American workers. Higher labor cost equals lower profit.

To the woke, lower profits are generally a good thing, except when the profits are theirs.

So! We had the head of a company in the public eye who, for the sake of maximizing his profits by using illegal cheap labor, was willing to call the president of the United States a racist for securing the nation's border. He did so by disingenuously pointing to rich Mexicans he wanted to soak in order to divert attention away from the poor ones he wanted to exploit.

He performed this bit of theater costumed in a cloak of moral superiority. Aspen's unthinking liberal white intelligentsia clapped like trained seals.

The applause might dwindle if Joe Biden's illegal immigrants were being flown to Aspen, as Tucker Carlson recommended and as they have been flown to Martha's Vineyard and other sanctuary cities that pretend to welcome them until they actually show up. But at least Kaplan would get that cheap labor he craves.

Then there's Gay Ski Week. SkiCo designates a special week each year for gay skiers. Gay skiers are not prohibited at other times, and straight skiers are not prohibited during Gay Ski Week, but the week is especially for gays. We are supposed to see their gayness the way we are supposed to see Blacks' skin color, sympathize with their lived experience, and heroize them. Don't dare tell them a restaurant doesn't open till 5:00 p.m., and don't tell them not to park in a no-parking zone.

SkiCo puts on this show, in part, to attract gay skiers. But gays are only about 2 percent of America (notwithstanding the average person's erroneous assumption that they are more like 20 percent, an assumption founded in their disproportionate numbers in woke advertising). Like Black skiers, gay skiers are a very small population (but we're working hard to increase their numbers!).

SkiCo's bigger purpose is to morally preen for the eyes of wealthy, straight, white liberals—their real customer base. Everyone is supposed to say, "Gays are great! Some of my best friends are gay, though I'm not gay myself, mind you. SkiCo is courageous and enlightened for having a Gay Ski Week. I think I'll get me another thirty-four-dollar hamburger and a bottle of Veuve Clicquot!"

I was once riding up the lift with a stranger during Gay Ski Week. He asked me, "Are you Albert?" Except that his pronunciation of "Albert" put the emphasis on the last syllable and dropped the "t" at the end. It came out more like "Al-BARE."

I always try to make our foreign visitors feel welcome and I wanted to do the same with this fellow from, I guessed, Argentina.

His "Al-BARE" was obviously a Spanish pronunciation of "Albert." As for the identity of this "Albert" for whom he mistook me, I had not a clue.

Keeping with my welcoming heart and always on the lookout to impress people with the multilingualism I perceive in myself, I answered him lovingly and intentionally even though he was not Black. I replied, "No, *me llama* Glenn."

"Hi, Glenn," he replied. "I was wondering if you're Al-BARE?" He remained in English, which was perfect, with no trace of an accent except for his Spanish pronunciation of "Albert."

His insistence on speaking English annoyed me slightly because it reminded me that whenever I am in a Spanish-speaking country, they always seem to prefer that we converse in English. In fact, they pretend not to understand my Spanish. I have concluded that people in Spanish-speaking countries don't speak Spanish at all. It's a big put-on.

In any event, I reasoned, I always have to speak English in their Spanish-speaking countries, so they should have to speak Spanish in my English-speaking one. I finally answered in the language he seemed to prefer, and very directly this time. "No. I'm Glenn, not Albert."

"No, no, no, no-no-no." He was chuckling and shaking his head. "I'm asking if you're a bear."

I looked at him, puzzled. "A bear?"

He glanced at the sky. "Never mind."

The encounter perplexed and mildly irritated me. But mindful of recent incidents of people being thrown off lifts by other riders for nothing more than commenting on snow depths up to their privates, I decided not to inquire further. We rode the rest of the way in silence.

I later described the odd encounter to a friend. The friend informed me of something that readers more sophisticated and hipper than I—which is to say, anyone born after about 1903—might already know. In gay vernacular, a "bear" is a gay man who is big and hairy. And maybe other things, too, but that is all I know about it.

The incident got me thinking. My would-be gay lover had ultimately concluded, correctly, that I am mostly ignorant about the ways of gays. But he didn't seem offended by my ignorance. He didn't demand that I learn such ways or practice such ways or that he be offered a "safe space" where he would not encounter people like me who are ignorant of such ways. He just chuckled, shrugged his shoulders, and went on his way, looking for a bear.

A lot has happened in society, gay-wise. Four generations ago, a gay act was a happy one. Two generations ago, a gay act was a criminal one. Now we have gay marriage. I don't oppose that. (But I do think that gays and the rest of us would have been better off if it had come about through a democratic process, as seemed inevitable until a swing-voting Supreme Court justice decided that he personally wanted to get credit for it.)

The changes have been sudden but mostly smooth. It says a lot about the goodness of the American people. In a country that is one of the most religious on earth, we have an amazing live-and-let-live attitude toward others of different religions, skin colors, and sexual persuasions.

Back to Gay Ski Week. I have no objection to it. But given the current societal acceptance of gays, it is a bit quaint and even condescending. It is a bit like, say, Scottish Ski Week. Or Black Ski Week.

Aspen engages in sanctimonious moral preening for causes that were won decades ago. It is no-risk establishmentarian brand-name edginess, which is to say it's not edgy at all. It is typical liberal faux-edginess.

Maybe SkiCo should put on a Global Warming Ski Week when everyone prays for a snow drought to publicize the impending global warming calamity. Instead, year after year, SkiCo touts Aspen's record-breaking snowfalls while shrieking that global warming could end it all tomorrow.

SkiCo's amateur approach to business and marketing is not typical for its owners, the astute Crown family. SkiCo is not the biggest jewel in the Crown's multibillion-dollar empire, so perhaps they don't pay enough attention to it. It shows in the way SkiCo company is run.

A few years ago at SkiCo, a huge employee theft scheme came to light. An executive named Derek Johnson and his wife had the authority to purchase skis for the company to use in rental operations and as demos. Over the course of twelve years, Johnson and his wife purchased double or triple the number of skis that the company needed and sold the extras on eBay. Johnson was on the Aspen City council for four of those years.

This was not small-time employee theft, like taking home ballpoint pens and batteries from the office supply room. Over the twelve-year period, Johnson stole about thirteen thousand pairs of high-end skis—over a thousand a year—with a total market value of about $6 million. Shamelessly, he was storing the skis he stole in a SkiCo warehouse, and he even billed the company for the boxes in which he fenced them to his customers.

This systematic multiyear scheme was notable mainly for the fact that it took that long for SkiCo to notice it. Johnson was disliked as a big bully at work, and that may be the only reason other employees finally stopped looking the other way.

Johnson served his sentence, was a model prisoner, and picked up some religion along the way. He has since returned to Aspen seeking to make amends and is working to pay off the restitution he owes SkiCo.

The point is not that Johnson is a good man who made a long-running mistake or a bad man who's still covering up that mistake—time will tell about that—but that SkiCo was running a pretty sloppy operation. In a letter to the judge after Johnson's conviction, SkiCo president Mike Kaplan said Johnson's theft was "unfathomable to me."

Much in the world is beyond Kaplan's fathoms. He's in over his head.

CHAPTER TEN

THE DEATH OF EXCELLENCE: THE ASPEN INSTITUTE DRIFTS LEFT

British journalist John O'Sullivan is noted for saying that any institution that is not explicitly conservative inevitably tends to drift left. The Aspen Institute affords a fine example of this principle in action.

From the outset, the teachers, staff, management, and students of the music component of the Aspen Institute frustrated the businessman in Walter Paepcke. After several years of conflicts, the parties effectuated a split of sorts. They set up a separate organization called Music Associates of Aspen to run the Aspen Music Festival and School, or AMFS. Paepcke gave them support in-kind in the form of facilities and publicity.

Paepcke's view of the musicians' business acumen proved prescient. For the next decades and into the present, AMFS struggled to make ends meet. They had always relied, in large part, on Aspenites to house the music students for free each summer, an arrangement that became especially unworkable during the COVID-19 pandemic.

They did secure funding to build a facility a couple of miles from Aspen on property donated to them by a Chicago real estate investor named Matthew Bucksbaum. They currently use that facility as a school each summer during the music festival, and Aspen Country Day School uses it the other three seasons as a prestigious private school. Even with this substantial asset, however, the costs of the AMFS operation far outstrip its revenues. They depend largely on charitable donations.

Some of the recent AMFS troubles are self-inflicted, a circumstance that Bucksbaum, who died in 2013, was fortunate not to witness. The school was founded as a classical music school by classical music lovers. But the current outspoken director, Alan Fletcher, often makes pronouncements that they intend to "diversify" their classical music. That is, they intend to second-chair traditional classical music in favor of the music of other—i.e., non-white—cultures.

As is always the case with woke virtue signaling, the signaling is as important as the virtue itself because the signaling permits the wokester to feel good about himself and receive applause from the wokerati.

To that end, Fletcher published an apologetic "Statement of Commitment," confessing that AMFS in the past had reflected "a society that privileges White talent and contributions." He explained that he and his lieutenants had attended remedial "racial literacy sessions" that "examined the intersections of Dr. Ibram Kendi's *How to Be an Antiracist*" and other critical race theory publications. The discussions were facilitated by a now-defunct

Pittsburgh outfit that made a good living by working that angle for a few years.

Fletcher's promises in his manifesto are quantified in a way that is easily interpreted as imposing racial quotas—the adoption of a formal and numerical policy of discrimination against white composers and musicians.

The facts that trouble Fletcher are not disputable, to be sure. It is a fact that white people have dominated classical music for centuries. They invented it and excelled at it—though, of course, they were not considered "white people" at the time, but Europeans of various nationalities.

On the other hand, a person walking around Aspen during the music festival to enjoy classical street music from AMFS musicians playing for tips will notice that the race—and aren't we supposed to notice race nowadays, as Fletcher, Kaplan, and their comrades urge?—of the violinists and cellists is disproportionately Asian. That fact seems to undercut Fletcher's premise that classical music is dominated by whites. The world's most famous cellist, Yo-Yo Ma, is Chinese.

On the *other* other hand, Asians are now considered white when it comes to reverse discrimination at such places as Harvard and Aspen. They call them "white adjacent" now. They do not count as people of color despite the color of their skin, apparently because they're not unsuccessful.

So, Fletcher is right after all. It is all in how you define race—is it by color or by conscience?

AMFS presents some jazz in addition to classical music. Fletcher made no apology for the near-absence of white jazz musicians and composers among the teachers and students of AMFS.

Fletcher's manifesto effectively redefines AMFS's definition of musical merit. It no longer means music composed and performed with excellence. It now means music composed and performed by people having the skin colors he deems excellent. This may bode badly for AMFS's weak finances when donors notice the shift.

The rest of the institute has survived better. After the music school split off from the institute but before he died in 1960, Walter Paepcke passed the reins to another Chicago friend, Robert O. Anderson, who held them for two decades. It was Anderson who donated the land for the AMFS facility. The son of a prominent Swedish immigrant banker, Anderson, like Paepcke, does not fit neatly into any category.

As a student at the University of Chicago, Anderson considered becoming a philosophy professor. Instead, his summer jobs in the Texas oil fields led him to wildcatting. He made several major finds and merged his company into Atlantic Richfield, where he rose to become president. At ARCO, he gambled and won big on the discovery of the vast oil field in Prudhoe Bay, Alaska. He was also an environmentalist who warned of the risks of global warming and was a Ronald Reagan Republican.

Anderson served as a trustee of Cal Tech. He was the biggest landowner in the United States, with over a million acres. And he was a petroleum engineering professor at the University of New Mexico.

Under Anderson's leadership, ARCO became a major collector of modern art. Like the Paepckes, he was also an admirer of Bauhaus design.

Anderson, and before him, the Paepckes, were thinkers, not tribalists. Their analytical skills usually led them to the correct conclusion, as shown by their extraordinary success in business and life. When they occasionally got something wrong, it was not because they were just following their tribe; it was because even a genius makes an occasional error.

In the 1970s, Anderson sought to build a hotel at the Aspen Meadows headquarters to lodge guests of the institute. When antidevelopment factions controlling city government thwarted his plan (there was no subsidized housing in it, after all), Anderson talked of moving the institute out of Aspen. Eventually, the headquarters did move to Maryland and later to Washington, DC. It subsequently grew less focused on Aspen and attendant cultural events like the Goethe and Bach festivals that launched in 1949 and 1950 and more like a national and international think tank.

O'Sullivan's posit that any organization not explicitly right-wing inevitably drifts leftward over time may apply to the institute. As think tanks go, its policy positions jibe more with the liberal Brookings Institution than the conservative Stanford-based Hoover. Today's Aspen Institute is clearly left-leaning, not wildly so but probably more than if it had eschewed the influence of the DC Beltway.

One of the most popular programs sponsored by the institute since 2005 is the Aspen Ideas Festival, a seminar of speakers and panelists. As O'Sullivan might have predicted, this ostensibly neutral organization is today largely run by Democrats who favor such speakers as Eric Holder, Hillary Clinton, Madeleine Albright, Ruth Bader Ginsburg, Joe Biden, and Barbra Streisand. "Balancing" them have not been serious conservatives like

Antonin Scalia, George W. Bush, Dick Cheney, Ted Cruz, or—needless to say—Donald Trump. Instead, the purported balance is supplied by the likes of Mitt Romney, Sandra Day O'Connor, and Paul Ryan. It is the hard, uncompromising Left versus squishy RINOs seeking approval from the DC cocktail party circuit.

After Anderson, the Aspen Institute was headed by Walter Isaacson for fifteen years until 2018. Isaacson is surely a Democrat, but he is no demagogue. He became head of CNN in 2001 when it was one of the great news organizations in the world, though even then, it was leaning to the left. To right the ship a bit, he sought meetings with Republicans about their concerns. For that, overtly leftist news organizations criticized him for "pandering" to the Republicans. We know what happened to CNN after he left in 2003 to come to the Aspen Institute.

Isaacson authored biographies of Albert Einstein and Benjamin Franklin that remain the gold standards, as well as a bestselling biography of Steve Jobs. The guy can write and think. He took seriously the responsibility to maintain the Aspen Institute as an independent, nonpartisan organization.

Isaacson was partially successful, but only partially. Although he was as good as one might hope for in such a position, during his reign, the institute continued to drift leftward, as big organizations invariably do.

Isaacson's successor is Daniel Porterfield, who started his career as deputy assistant secretary for public affairs in President Clinton's Health and Human Services Department. Then he started up the ladder of academia, culminating with the presidency of a small Pennsylvania college called Franklin and Marshall. To enroll a more diverse student body, Porterfield granted many tuition discounts proportionate to skin pigmentation. That strained the college finances. After he left to come to the Aspen Institute, deep budget cuts were necessary for the college to continue operations.

Porterfield made a notable public relations mistake during COVID-19. The institute applied for and was granted about $10 million in COVID-19 relief money. This was for a charitable organization with liquid assets totaling at least thirty times that. After a public outcry, the institute returned the money. But applying for it to begin with reflected a bad error in judgment and a money-grubbing mentality that the Paepckes, Anderson, and Isaacson would have abhorred.

A branch of the institute is the Aspen Network of Development Entrepreneurs. The mission and website of ANDE read well enough. They aim to "provide critical financial, educational, and business support services to small and growing businesses (SGBs) based on the conviction that SGBs will create jobs, stimulate long-term economic growth, and produce environmental and social benefits."

In practice, these high-minded ideals mean something other than entrepreneurism. Much of the work of ANDE is focused on such topics as "Entrepreneur Women and Local Development in Rural Mexico Areas," "Digital, Diverse, and Going Global: A New Dawn for Women-Led Firms," "Advancing Women's Empowerment Fund" and "How to Invest with a Gender Lens."

Not everything has lurched leftward at the institute. Another branch is called Ascend, which is dedicated to promoting family cohesion. Their work emphasizes Black and Native American families.

One might argue that emphasizing Blacks and Native Americans constitutes a form of reverse discrimination, but perhaps that is where their work is most needed. When the Black illegitimacy rate is over triple that of whites, and in major cities, most Black pregnancies end in abortion, it makes sense that efforts to foster family cohesion would focus first on Blacks.

With subgroups such as Ascend, the institute is still not a monolithic left-leaning organization. But the uppermost leadership increasingly subordinates ideological diversity to the racial and sexual kind—which is often hostile to the ideological kind. In doing so, they risk their credibility as a forum for ideas and merit.

At this rate of drift, within a few more years, the Aspen Institute will bash into the sharp and unforgiving rocks of wokeness. Then the institute will look like today's punitive, censorious, and intolerant college campuses. It will transform from an intellectual endeavor seeking truth into a cheap, propagandizing show that force-feeds preconceived "truths."

CHAPTER ELEVEN

HIGH ATTITUDE: IS IT END TIMES FOR *THE ASPEN TIMES*?

Aspen Mountain today is mostly accessed via the high-speed gondola at the base, adjacent to the SkiCo-owned Little Nell Hotel. But historically, the access was a few blocks away at the base of an old low-speed lift called Lift 1A. That lift still runs, slow as ever. The rest of the site is now a collection of worn-out buildings and run-down facilities peppered with some modern luxury townhomes.

There has been talk for years about replacing the old lift with a new high-speed lift or gondola and building a modestly sized luxury hotel on the site. Access to the mountain would be improved, and pressure would be taken off the existing gondola at the main access point adjacent to the Little Nell Hotel a few hundred yards away. The new hotel would pose some competition to the Little Nell, which would be a good thing.

The proposed redevelopment was reasonable in scope, tastefully designed, and respectful of the history of the site. The developers—a group of longtime Aspen businessmen—even promised to build a ski museum there. The new lift would extend farther down the mountain so skiers could hop on it from a downtown street and, at the end of the day, ski right into town.

I lived for five years just two blocks above the site. The proposal to extend the lift down the hill and into town would have increased my "commute" to the boarding point, but it would be all downhill on skis, something that seems tolerable when you're embarking on a day of downhill skiing. Most of my neighbors thought the proposal was a good one.

The reflexively antidevelopment Aspen lefties disagreed. The developer intended to make a profit on his risk and his investment, after all, and so that was bad. After years of debate, the project was finally put to the voters. Over the Left's objections, voters narrowly passed it.

After the redevelopment was approved, the developers sold the land in 2021 to another potential developer for a handsome profit. That is not unusual in Aspen. But the antidevelopment crowd screamed. Too much profit, too fast, they cried. And the sale jeopardized the redevelopment that they had opposed!

The anti-developers ginned up some rationales for their revived opposition to the redevelopment. Since the people of Aspen had already voted for it, the opponents put aside the merits of the redevelopment and instead went after the people involved.

One member of the ownership group that sold the property to the new potential redeveloper was Jeff Gorsuch, a member of the prominent Gorsuch family, which goes back about five generations in Colorado. This particular Gorsuch was the owner of an iconic clothing store in Aspen for the last fifty years, as well as one in Vail. For that, it is hard to criticize him even if you're an antibusiness nut.

But Gorsuch had a weak spot that could be exploited. He was a distant cousin of Supreme Court Justice Neil Gorsuch, whom leftie Aspenites deem a racist, homophobic Trump appointee who stole his appointment via procedural gymnastics and legal wrangling. Never mind that Justice Gorsuch joined the liberal wing of the court in casting the deciding vote on the 2020 decision protecting gays and transexuals under the Civil Rights Act and even wrote the court's opinion. Insofar as the Left of Aspen was concerned, all that mattered was that he was a Trump appointee.

Orange Man Bad. And so must be his judicial appointees, such as Neil Gorsuch. And so must be the distant cousins of his appointees, such as the other Gorsuch who was part of the Aspen development group. A local civic leader red spray-painted a Gorsuch store window with "GO BACK TO VAIL." For that vandalism, *The Aspen Times* wrote a sympathetic piece—on the vandal, not the victim.

Then there is the person Gorsuch and his partners sold the property to, who also had a weak spot to exploit. He's Russian, and the sale occurred just weeks after the Russian invasion of Ukraine.

The Aspen Left thus had their hook. An old-time retired/unretired *Aspen Times* columnist who should have known better wrote an unflattering column about the sale in which he explicitly and wrongly called the buyer a "Russian oligarch."

"Russian oligarch" has a particular meaning these days. It suggests a Russian who has grown rich through shady connections with the corrupt Russian government. The column was biased, inflammatory, bigoted, and poorly reasoned clickbait that stoked political fires by impugning a person's integrity on the basis of his national origin.

American lawyers for the Russian demanded a retraction. They pointed out that their client was not tied to Putin and, in fact, had denounced the Russian invasion of Ukraine. He was not even one of the Russians who had been sanctioned by the West. Being a rich Russian guy does not make their client a "Russian oligarch" any more than being a rich American makes someone an "American oligarch."

The Aspen Times belatedly recognized their unfair column and sloppy editing. They published a correction changing the description from "Russian oligarch" to "Russian billionaire." But they continued to bash the Russian and the property sale to him. The Russian and his lawyers continued to object to that bashing. The Russian finally sued *The Aspen Times* for defamation.

This drama took place during a transition in ownership at *The Aspen Times*. The newspaper had been owned for years by a small newspaper conglomerate called Swift Communications. Swift was then bought by a larger conglomerate named Ogden Newspapers. It is a fifth-generation family-owned company from West Virginia.

Unusual for the newspaper business, the new owners are conservatives. And unusual for conservatives who dare enter Aspen, they did not try to disguise that fact, though they did not advertise it either. Worst of all, in the minds of the staff at *The Aspen Times*, the new owners seemed to think they were the boss just because they were the owners.

The new owners wisely wanted to settle the lawsuit with the Russian. They entered into negotiations with the Russian through his lawyers to accomplish that.

During the sensitive negotiations, the new owners asked the newspaper staff not to write anything further about the matter. This is standard in settlement negotiations, especially in this kind of case. When the plaintiff alleges that the defendant repeatedly has defamed him and continues to do so, it is prudent for the defendant to keep quiet while the parties try to work things out.

The staff refused to follow the new owners' instructions during the sensitive settlement negotiations. After the old-time retired/unretired columnist started the dispute by wrongly calling the Russian an oligarch, another longtime columnist joined the action.

Roger Marolt, whose two brothers reside in the taxpayer-subsidized housing projects, wrote a piece critical of the Russian and his property purchase. The new owners refused to publish it. Marolt then wrote another column criticizing the newspaper for refusing to publish his first column. Still in settlement negotiations, the owners refused to publish that as well. Thwarted in publicly criticizing the newspaper he worked for, Marolt or someone else evidently leaked it on social media.

Marolt is not a lawyer, but he is no rube. He apparently runs a little bookkeeping/accounting/tax-preparing firm. He should be sophisticated enough about money, if not law, to realize that his selfish antics were putting at risk the existence of the newspaper—then in delicate negotiations with a billionaire who could squash them like a bug—and the local jobs that he pretends to champion.

Weeks later, the parties reached a settlement. Marolt wrote yet another column. *The Aspen Times* editor, Andrew Travers, published that one without gaining permission from the new owners. Travers apparently contends that he had some kind of implicit permission, but evidently, the new owners didn't see it that way. They fired Travers on the spot.

Travers had lasted only a few days on the job. His predecessor, David Krause, had already been pushed out. Krause, a former sports page reporter in Denver who had relocated to Aspen a few years ago in the hope of scoring some taxpayer-subsidized housing (he never did), was the guy who sent me the nastygram email on Christmas Eve terminating my column a couple of years earlier.

At the news of Krause being pushed out, I thought (but did not say): "Aspen, it's not for everyone. Maybe you should move on."

Some of the other staff resigned or were pushed out in the wake of the firing of Travers. Marolt quit and went to work for the competing newspaper because he did not like writing for a paper where the editors might edit him. At the new newspaper, he wrote a column explaining that he had literally cried over the affair.

Marolt seems oblivious to matters of money for a guy who apparently makes a living as a bookkeeper/tax preparer. In a more recent column, he expressed his wish that visitors would stop coming to Aspen. (Maybe they should just mail their money in.) But his leftist illogic undoubtedly succeeded in making him feel good—which is always their main goal. He gleefully expressed his ignorant hate for the hands that feed him while basking in the approval of his fellow travelers in that hate.

Liberals conveniently confuse strong feelings—typically feelings of hate—with a strong argument. This is what sends them into the streets to smash windows and hurl Molotov cocktails. It justifies canceling speakers and writers with whom they disagree. The Left's conflation of reason with emotion produces a conflagration of hateful rage interspersed with crying jags like the one Marolt bragged about, every one of which they enjoy because it seems to them that crying makes them right and, even better, makes them victims.

During the pandemic, conservative activist Candace Owens was an outspoken critic of the government's COVID-19 policy and expressed doubt about the efficacy of COVID-19 tests and masks, sentiments that later proved scientifically legitimate. She visited Aspen in September 2021. Despite her doubts, she did the responsible thing in arranging a COVID-19 test because proof of a negative result was required for admission to some of the public forums she planned to attend. This was back before at-home test kits.

The Aspen testing laboratory recognized her name and knew of her conservative politics. In an email to Owens, they criticized her views on COVID-19 and righteously refused to administer the test to her. This put at risk not just Owens but everyone with whom she came in contact.

The testing lab's only defense for this stunt was no defense at all. They implied that they were the victims in refusing to test her because they didn't anticipate that Owens would reveal their refusal. They never did admit their mistake.

In short, they expressed their petulant anger at someone who dared to have views to which they objected by withholding medical services for the benefit of Aspen as a whole. They told themselves this was the right thing to do because, well, it felt righteous and good. Then they cast themselves as the victims because they got caught. Meanwhile, the true victim, Candace Owens, laughed the matter off and declined to pursue legal action.

The incident became a mini-controversy in Aspen. The few conservatives in town argued that it was wrong for a public medical facility to jeopardize the health of an individual and the public at large by denying services to her on the basis of her politics. The liberals argued that it was not wrong at all. They were willing to risk the health of the public with what they themselves characterized as a deadly danger as a price for the feel-good of hating and punishing Owens for her view that it was not.

The Aspen Times covered for the lab by suggesting that the parties disagreed about the relevant facts. As in…move on, nothing to see here, and even if there were, it's all blurry. That's bull. The pertinent facts are undisputed—the parties' communications are in written emails.

Speaking of melodramatic crying jags, celebrating supposed victimhood, and telling lies to punish people for their politics, Andrew Travers—that fired editor of *The Aspen Times*—wrote a one-sided article about the fubar/snafu/clusterfuck firing that he and the other writers and editors had brought on themselves. Published in *The Atlantic*, the title was "End Times for Aspen." The article was subtitled, "How a Soviet-born developer and a West Virginia billionaire destroyed a 141-year-old Colorado newspaper."

In his *Atlantic* article, Travers regularly repeats this "Soviet-born" ditty as if the Russian was personal friends with Lenin and Stalin. Travers seems to think he is getting the last laugh by taking a swipe that falls just short of "Russian oligarch," the particular phrase that, as Travers and *The Atlantic* know, might get them sued.

The Russian is indeed "Soviet-born" in the sense that everyone born in the Soviet Union prior to its collapse in 1990 is, including today's Ukrainians. But the government running his country at the time he was born has little relevance to the subject at hand. It's just a cheap shot.

In fairness to Travers, however, this swipe at the Soviet Union is probably the only one he has ever made at them.

As for his reference to the "West Virginia billionaire," he apparently assumes that a West Virginia domicile makes the new owner a redneck, perhaps in league with that traitor Joe Manchin, or associated with a wretched coal-mining hellhole rather than being the publisher of dozens of small newspapers around the country.

Travers would do well to recall that long before John Denver wrote "Rocky Mountain High," he wrote "Country Road," in which he sang that West Virginia is "almost heaven." But the Left in Aspen is too busy imagining with John Lennon that there is no heaven. It's easy if they try.

Travers explains in the body of his article that the new owners of *The Aspen Times* got off to a bad start when one of them mentioned a skiing article he had written for another newspaper that contained the line "powder sucks." According to Travers, that "did not endear him to our team." In an interesting projection, he also concluded that the new guy who offended the "team" with his quip about powder skiing was thin-skinned. It goes downhill from there.

The Aspen establishment piled on. A collection of eighteen city council types, county commissioners, and, naturally, former mayor Mick Ireland wrote a letter to the new owners of *The Aspen Times*. In their letter, they demanded that the fired editor be reinstated, demanded control over future editorial decisions at the newspaper, and explicitly threatened to punish the newspaper if their demands were not met. In short, government officials and bureaucrats overtly demanded content control over the newspaper on penalty of governmental sanctions.

In view of their insistence on the government having editorial control over the newspaper, it is ironic that their grievance was the newspaper's own exercise of editorial control over itself. Censorship at private companies is apparently OK, but only if it is done not by the company itself but by leftists acting under the auspices of the government. You have no right to control what you say. Only the government has that right.

Their demand for a rehiring of these editors and writers who had been terminated for bad writing, bad editing, insubordination, and fouling up sensitive settlement negotiations with a billionaire, was in marked contrast to what happened when *The Aspen Times* fired me for my "values" and opinions they didn't like. Nothing happened then. They made not a peep. I was fair game because I was a conservative.

To the credit of the new owners of *The Aspen Times*, they have not given in to the mob's demands. But the lefties have a card up their sleeves, or so they think. They are urging the local leftie billionaires to buy the newspaper back from the new owners so that they can once again make it their propagandizing Pravda. So far, no takers. These billionaires may be lefties, but they did not become billionaires by being stupid.

Travers concluded his *Atlantic* article with a warning that what happened in Aspen could happen elsewhere. I don't disagree. It can—and it should.

When a media outlet publishes defamatory material, it should be held accountable in a court of law. The law of defamation is not censorship. It is a set of legal principles going back centuries intended to protect people from scurrilous and injurious falsehoods. Society is reasonable in asking the media especially not to spread falsehoods, given the power they have and their professional and ethical obligation to the truth. In communications to the masses, the media has a special obligation to be honest and fair, not a special immunity from being dishonest and unfair.

The media has lost sight of that. Not just CNN and *The Aspen Times* but some of the conservative outlets as well. This has escalated military style, with each side contending that its atrocities are justified and even necessary because the other side does it. The result is that the media is held in low esteem today across the board. People do not believe what the media tells them because so often it is false or misleading. Fortunately, this means that people do not so easily believe the falsehoods propagated by the media (unless they already agree with the narrative the falsehoods support). But unfortunately, they do not believe the truths either. When the media mixes lies with truths, nobody believes anything, and everyone is ill-informed. The media could save their profession and perhaps the world by recommitting to their sacred role as the Fourth Estate.

I played with the title of Travers' article for the title of this chapter purely for the purpose of irony. OK, not so much irony as mockery. Contrary to the thrust of Traver's article, *The Aspen Times* is not ending, notwithstanding the sinister dealings of that "Soviet-born developer" and "West Virginia billionaire."

The Aspen Times has so far survived its self-inflicted wounds. It will continue to survive for exactly so long as real estate brokers use it to advertise $10 million houses—not a minute less and not a minute more. The internet has devasted newspapers throughout the world. This particular newspaper has bucked the trend, not because it had brilliant writing and reporting but because it had a brilliant real estate market. Any notion to the contrary is delusionary conceit.

So no, *The Aspen Times* will not end under its new conservative ownership simply because the employment of a particular leftie editor ended in record time, despite the predictions and wishes of that editor in a fawning leftie rag like *The Atlantic*. *The Aspen Times* survived the loss of its most popular columnist in its 140-year history—yours truly. Surely, it will now survive the loss of that insubordinate editor.

The advertising gravy train does have an end in sight, however. Realtors in Aspen say their newspaper ads seldom land them buyers, sellers, or prospects. As they do everywhere, people in Aspen now shop for houses on the internet. The reason the realtors run newspaper ads anyway is to impress their clients that they are doing something to earn their six- and seven-figure commissions besides driving people around in Jaguar SUVs. That will end in Aspen, just as it is ending everywhere else, but it will take a few more years simply because rich homebuyers like being driven around in Jaguar SUVs.

Whether Aspen itself will survive is another question.

CHAPTER TWELVE

PARADISE LOST: THE END OF ASPEN?

A few Aspen organizations remain mostly unconquered by the wokesters. That may be because their members travel outside the woke universe. Two stand out. Both are unrelated to the Aspen Institute. They could serve as examples for the salvation of this former paradise.

The first is the Aspen Center for Physics. The center was formed in 1962 by physicist, businessman, founder of the Woody Creek Tavern, friend (weirdly) of Hunter Thompson, renaissance man, and inheritor of the Champion Spark plug fortune, George Stranahan.

Stranahan died in 2021 and had limited involvement in the center even before his death. But the governance of the center has always comprised world-class physicists, as have its participants. According to their website, sixty-four Nobel Laureates and sixty-five countries have participated in the center's activities. Over ten thousand scientific journal articles have cited the center for contributions in particle physics, condensed matter physics, astrophysics, cosmology, biophysics, mathematics, gravitational wave physics, nonlinear dynamics, and other related sciences. Over one thousand scientists a year participate in its seminars and meetings.

Apart from their important but obtuse scientific seminars, they also offer public lectures on such topics as "Gravitational Wave Observatories," "Adaptive Matter," and "Supermassive Black Holes."

The center has published no statement of commitment asking the physical world to yield to the diverse one. At the center, other than perhaps in their mysterious world of quantum mechanics, two plus two still equals four.

To be sure, the website does boast that while only 12 percent of physicists are women, the percentage at the center is more like 15 percent. I wonder if they are truly boasting about the difference between 12 percent and 15 percent as only a physicist might, or if they are being a bit funny with some physicist humor.

Back in the '90s, they put on a "Focal Week on Women in Physics" that is slightly reminiscent of SkiCo's Gay and Black Ski Weeks. But later, they apparently discarded the quaint and condescending notion that women need special promotion to succeed the way SkiCo thinks Blacks and gays do. The logic and data-gathering traits of a physicist will have that effect. And, so far, the center's president has not sent around a memo to employees telling them that some of his best friends are women physicists and dictating how to behave around these exotic creatures. In sum, the center is still compact, efficient, innovative, merit-based, and, consequently, well-regarded.

The second organization that has stayed true to its mission for over fifty years is Mountain Rescue Aspen, about which I have some personal knowledge. MRA is a 100 percent volunteer organization dedicated to search and rescue in Pitkin County. Of its fifty members, ten have served for more than twenty-five years, and the average length of service is twelve years. On average, they spend five hours a week, amounting to over 250 hours a year, on training and have conducted over one hundred search and rescue missions. Some spend more like one thousand hours a year. Many have been injured on missions, and none receive a penny for their service. They even buy their own outdoor clothing.

They don't do it for glory; these people don't signal their virtue. MRA rules prohibit the identification of members who participate in any given mission even if—especially if—they do something heroic, as they often do.

With lives at stake, MRA does not obsess with guilt trips, diversity crap, or identity politics. They don't care about the skin color or sexual proclivities of their members. They don't care about the economic class of their members—they have multimillionaires, small business owners, former Wall Street types, and blue-collar tradesmen. They have people living in Aspen mansions and people living in house trailers. What they care about is skill, conditioning, judgment, reliability, and teamwork.

This is shown by the role of the women, who comprise a fair if not "equitable" percentage of the MRA membership. Many of these women are valued, strong, highly skilled mountaineers who make important contributions to the team.

But a fit woman is not as physically strong—especially in brute muscle strength—as a fit man. This is common knowledge.

It is part of what the wokesters would call your "lived experience" in contexts where it supports their narrative.

In athletics, the different strength of men and women has been recognized for as long as there has been athletic competition. That is why athletic competitions are usually divided by sex, at least until recently when men unable to beat other men have started pretending to be women, which will continue until it becomes apparent that women's sports are being sacrificed on the altar of crossdressers.

That women generally are less physically strong than men does not make women inferior, and it doesn't make me bad for reporting it. It is simply a fact.

Wokesters do not like this fact. Wokesters are uncomfortable with physical variances between the sexes even as they cubbyhole personality variances. They think the sex of children with two X chromosomes, who have always been called "girls," cannot include tomboys, and so they must have their breasts amputated and be deemed boys. They think the sex of children with a Y chromosome, who have always been called "boys," cannot include ones that like to play with dolls, so they must have their genitals cut off and be deemed girls.

They similarly think "humans" cannot include women who are less physically strong than men. And so, the strength tests proving that fact must be abolished.

They have lately bullied the military into loosening physical strength tests for women even beyond the inherent effect of using strength tests that are proportionate to body size, such as pullups and pushups. Let's hope that on the battlefield, our enemies will similarly test our women soldiers less physically than they test our men soldiers.

When I was a member of MRA, nature's bias against women in the field of brute physical strength was never a sore point. It was accepted as a reality that we dealt with in a way suited to each mission. On lost-person searches and even on missions requiring technical rock-climbing skills, women often held integral or leading roles. On body recoveries, on the other hand, where a heavy deadweight sometimes must be transported considerable distances, women were hardly ever in the lead.

I was on a body recovery mission in 2012 with two strong and highly skilled mountaineers in the Bell Cord Couloir separating the picturesque North and South Maroon Peaks near Aspen—one of the most photographed mountain scenes in the world. The rugged couloir is a steep, loose, ice-paved death trap that channels falling rocks and boulders and accelerates them to ballistic velocities. It has claimed novices and experts alike. You can do everything right and still die in the couloir.

That was the case with the victim whose body we recovered that day. Traversing between the North and South Bells, he had been knocked into the top of the couloir by a falling half-ton boulder the size of an oven. He slid and tumbled six hundred vertical feet before being caught by the bergschrund separating the ice face from the rock wall. He was probably dead before his body came to rest.

A Blackhawk helicopter dropped off our rescue team at the base of the couloir. And I mean "dropped." In heavy rescue gear, we jumped five feet out of the hovering helicopter onto a steep talus field.

Three of us, including me, were chosen to ascend to the victim about one thousand vertical feet up the couloir. The leader was an excellent local mountaineering guide, and the other was another longtime member of MRA whom I'll call "Harold."

The couloir's incline is over forty-five degrees and was hard, wet ice that day. We wore crampons on our boots and carried ice axes, of course, but a slip onto the ice would be perilous. If we were unable to arrest our fall using our ice axes within a few feet, we would be goners. Imagine a hockey puck on a frozen waterfall.

We finally reached the victim in the evening and, with a lot of effort, hauled the battered body out of the bergschrund. But a problem presented: How do we get the body down the couloir? The couloir was too narrow to get the Blackhawk in. And a longline from a Blackhawk hovering hundreds of feet above the couloir would be dicey. We did not even have a body bag on hand, because we were unaware that the man was dead until we reached him.

Harold then did something amazing. He wrapped the body in an emergency nylon tent and then tied up the packaged body with one end of a spare rope. He tied the other end to himself.

We also still had our separate team rope. On that rope, Harold would be the low man in charge of managing the body package. The expert mountaineering team leader would be the high man managing the team rope and the belays—a feat in itself. I tied into the middle of the rope and didn't do much.

The body package was two hundred pounds of deadweight. Harold positioned it downhill from himself, edged into the steep couloir, and began a side-stepping descent. The idea was that the package below him would slide down the slope. Gravity was our friend.

And our enemy. The descending package exerted a massive jerky downhill force as it bounced over the steep, rough ice and off the sheer rock sidewalls of the couloir. Stowing his ice axe, Harold held the package rope firmly in both hands and dug his crampons into the rotten ice. Bereft of his axe, a single slip could have been catastrophic to everything attached to the rope—the body package, Harold, me, and the team leader. We would slide, tumble, and fall a thousand feet, and our bodies would be recovered in pieces, if at all.

But Harold didn't slip. We descended in the dark for hours. From twenty feet above, my eyes were glued to Harold's every move, partly to give him the benefit of my headlamp but mostly because I was scared shitless. I prayed that he was as surefooted as he seemed. He astonished me with his selfless exhibition of problem-solving, brute strength, courage, phenomenal endurance, balletic balance, and true grit. It was pure Harold. That night, he brought me out to where he lived his life—out on the edge.

A few years later, Harold and another MRA member were caught in an avalanche near Aspen. The other member survived and reported Harold's last words as the avalanche swept over them: "We're gonna take a ride!"

I doubt any woman could have done what Harold did on that recovery mission in the couloir—nor could many men. No woman I have met has that combination of physical strength and defiant, dangerous testosterone. MRA wanted a few people like Harold around, and I'm sure they still do. For MRA, it is all about the mission.

Mountain Rescue Aspen and the Aspen Center for Physics have missions that are very different, though equally important. One is to save lives, and the other is to understand the universe. Both have plenty of members of various sexual orientations, skin colors, and political persuasions—left, right, and in between. But on this, they agree: merit matters.

What happened to Aspen was perhaps inevitable. It happens in almost all glitzy, rich resort towns, including Martha's Vineyard, Nantucket, Carmel, Lake Tahoe, and a hundred others. What happened is the decadent, leftward drift that afflicts most societies in the way John O'Sullivan observed. Human institutions freed from workaday worries become places not to work or live but to play.

The Left specializes in play. From an early age and all the way through college, they have liberal teachers, many of whom were attracted to their professions, in part because it gave them lots of holidays and summers off to play. To validate their own choice, some teachers teach their students the same value—the value not to value true value.

It's not a hard lesson to teach, or to learn, even though the lesson is false. Over the course of a long weekend or a two-week vacation, play seems more fun than work or life. Two weeks in Italy is obviously more exciting than two weeks in the office cubicle. It's easy and moderately interesting, and the food and scenery are great. There is no hard work to do, and there are usually no serious problems or conflicts to solve. It's life at the amusement park, one ride after another. Forget that the rides are forgettable. They're fun, and that's what matters.

The Left tells itself that this play is not only good in itself but also their life of goodness. They expressly set their play—their "life"—in opposition to their work. This is seen in their constant loud refrain about balancing work with life—as if work is something that is separate from and interferes with life.

Conservatives, in contrast, are usually unburdened by much play. Conservatives usually enjoy their work, especially if it is useful to others. Conservatives do not try to "balance" work against life any more than they try to "balance" family against life; they see work and family as equal parts of life, allies to life, and essentials to life. That's why conservatives are typically good at all three: work, family, and life.

Polls consistently show conservatives are happier for this. They are happier not despite their hard work and family commitments but largely because of them.

Conservatives know that the "life" the Left believes work interferes with is not really life at all. It's just the Left's amusement park rides. But skiing backward, bicycling, drinking, snorting, eating, and bathroom gunplay are not life. Life is work, achievement, love, courage, exploration, honesty, and generosity. Life is not all about you and your sandbox. It's about other people, things, and values outside your sandbox.

Don't think I believe I've excelled in these qualities I promote—work, achievement, love, courage, exploration, honesty, and generosity. But as I tell my grown children, there are worse sins than hypocrisy. At least I am honest that I accidentally practice bad while preaching good.

Rich resort towns like Aspen become decadent dens of leftists because they deliberately and dishonestly chase the bad at the expense of the good. Too many rich people with too much time on their hands and too few values in their hearts take up residence there. They seek amusement park fun in elaborate but little ways.

Too many rent-seeking remoras hang around to sponge off those rich people, envying and trying to emulate their life of play even as they hate them for it.

When they succeed at amusement but fail at happiness, as they usually do, they double down. They seldom look into their empty hearts because it takes real courage to look there and real work to fix what they would see and not see. They're not good at either—courage or work—because they have practiced them so little. They're not grown-ups. They're children looking for another amusing distraction on the playground.

Meanwhile, to validate their emptiness, they attack conservatives who have found fulfillment in living human lives. Conservatives' work ethic is deemed greed. Conservatives' family lives are deemed racist. Conservatives' wealth is deemed obscene. Conservatives' generosity is deemed insufficient. Conservatives' happiness may appear genuine, but that's because they're just too stupid to know better—as shown by their stupid religious beliefs.

Unsurprisingly, many conservatives don't frequently go to these liberal places where their lives, work, family, wealth, generosity, and happiness are attacked. Devoid of real diversity and culture, these places spiral down into boring monochromatic gray leftism like Soviet-style apartment buildings in suburban Moscow. At the extreme end of this process—achieved some time ago in Aspen—conservatives in these authoritarian wastelands are viewed as subhumans deserving of cancellation, if not extermination.

And so the Left wins. But in the end, their victory is Pyrrhic. They enjoy their pleasurable feelings of moral superiority just as they enjoy their other games and play, but pleasure is not the same as satisfaction. Humans are not built for nonstop enjoyment any more than they're built for gluttony.

Like gluttony, however, play is seductive—and addictive. People who become unhappy and unhealthy from gluttony, drugs, and other vices think the cure for their unhappiness must be more of the same. They confuse pleasure with happiness. This is a common affliction in modern man.

When a wise thirty-three-year-old declared his nascent nation's independence a couple of centuries ago, he wrote of a God-given right to pursue happiness in conjunction with a concomitant right to life and liberty. He was not writing about skiing, drugs, gourmet meals, or endless play. He was writing about living an examined life—a life of merit, achievement, dedication, and service, a life of truth, justice, and beauty, a life that Thomas Jefferson himself exemplified.

That, my friends, is what the Paepckes, Anderson, Pfeifer, and, yes, Isaacson and Harold knew and what many of us have forgotten. I pray we relearn it before it's too late.

ACKNOWLEDGMENTS

The author gratefully acknowledges the assistance and support of Kingsley Browne, Jim Jenista, Chad ("Bitter") Klinger, a good friend who chooses not to be acknowledged but knows who he is, and, very importantly, my excellent editor at Post Hill Press, Adam Bellow.

ABOUT THE AUTHOR

Glenn K. Beaton was a token conservative columnist at the Aspen Times for seven years before being fired one Christmas Eve because, to their dismay, he had become the most popular columnist in the 140-year history of the newspaper. His column often generated more clicks than frontpage news. Since then, he's taken his show on the road and has nearly a million readers on his blog, theaspenbeat.com.

In previous lives, Glenn practiced law at the Supreme Court, was an aerospace engineer for Boeing, and worked as a roustabout in an oil field. He is an accomplished amateur mountaineer who summited the Eiger and the Matterhorn and was a Full Member of Mountain Rescue Aspen where he participated in numerous hiking, mountaineering, avalanche, helicopter, rescue, and body recovery missions.

Made in the USA
Middletown, DE
21 April 2023